Roots of Wellness

Nurturing Health and Sustainability at Home

By Donald V. Dunham

Published by DBUGKING

Illustrations by DBUGKING

For more information and the companion site for the books, please visit

http://premiumgourmetandfunctionalmushrooms.com

Printed in the United States of America

First Printing, 2024

(DBUGKING) AKA Donald V Dunham

In support of the Exit Ranch Functional Mushroom and Herb Farm.

A DBUGKING "business for cause".

OpenAI. (2023). ChatGPT (September 25 Version) [Large

language model]. https://chat.openai.com

Table of Contents

Introduction

In a world where the pace of life can be hectic and our connection to nature often takes a back seat, there is a growing movement toward transforming our living spaces into havens of health and sustainability. Welcome to the concept of an organic in-home environment—a mindful approach to living that seeks to harmonize our daily lives with the principles of nature.

Imagine a home where every element, from the food on your plate to the materials in your furnishings, is chosen with a conscious commitment to health and environmental well-being. This is more than a trend; it's a holistic lifestyle that recognizes the interconnectedness of personal wellness and the health of our planet.

What is an Organic In-Home Environment?

An organic in-home environment is more than just a collection of eco-friendly products or a focus on chemical-free cleaning. It's a comprehensive approach that extends into every corner of your living space. It's about cultivating a sanctuary that not only supports your well-being but also treads lightly on the Earth.

Prioritizing Organic Food and Gardening

At the heart of this concept is the idea of organic living, beginning with the food we nourish ourselves with. Picture a kitchen filled with fresh, locally sourced, and seasonal organic produce. Beyond this, envision a small garden patch in your backyard or a cluster of pots on your windowsill, where you can cultivate your own herbs and vegetables, ensuring that every meal is a celebration of health and sustainability.

Mindful Cleaning and Sustainable Practices

But it's not just about what you eat; it's about every facet of your home. An organic in-home environment extends to the cleaning products you use, favoring natural and eco-friendly solutions. It embraces energy-efficient practices, waste reduction, and a commitment to sustainable design. Think of it as a conscious effort to minimize your ecological footprint while maximizing your well-being.

Creating a Sanctuary for Health and Harmony

Ultimately, an organic in-home environment is about creating a sanctuary—a space where you can thrive physically, mentally, and emotionally. It's an invitation to weave the principles of nature into the fabric of your daily life, fostering not just a house but a holistic, health-conscious home.

Join us on a journey to explore the roots of wellness, as we delve into the practical steps, insights, and inspirations that can help you cultivate an organic haven within your own four walls. Welcome to the transformative world of living organically at home.

Choosing Organic Practices for Health, Sustainability, and Overall Well-being

In our quest for a fulfilling and healthy life, the choices we make within the walls of our homes play a pivotal role. Embracing organic practices isn't just a lifestyle trend; it's a conscious decision with far-reaching impacts on our well-being and the sustainability of the planet we call home. Let's delve into why choosing organic practices is crucial for health, sustainability, and overall well-being.

**1. Health Benefits:

- **Nutrient-Rich Foods:** Organic farming methods prioritize soil health, resulting in nutrient-dense crops. Choosing organic means nourishing your body with food that is richer in vitamins, minerals, and antioxidants.
- **Reduced Exposure to Harmful Chemicals:** Conventional farming often involves the use of pesticides and synthetic fertilizers. Opting for organic food reduces your exposure to these potentially harmful chemicals, promoting a healthier immune system and reducing the risk of pesticide-related health issues.

**2. Environmental Sustainability:

- **Preserving Soil Health:** Organic farming techniques focus on maintaining soil fertility through natural practices such as crop rotation and composting. This not only ensures the health of the soil but also contributes to long-term agricultural sustainability.
- **Conserving Water Resources:** Organic farming generally requires less water than conventional methods. By choosing organic products, you indirectly contribute to the conservation of water resources, an increasingly critical concern in many regions.

**3. Reducing Environmental Impact:

- **Minimizing Chemical Runoff:** Chemical runoff from conventional farming can contaminate water sources and harm ecosystems. Organic practices, with their reduced reliance on synthetic chemicals, contribute to a cleaner and healthier environment.
- **Mitigating Climate Change:** Organic farming often involves carbon sequestration practices, helping to mitigate the effects of climate change. By choosing organic, you align your lifestyle choices with a more sustainable and climate-friendly approach.

**4. Overall Well-being:

- **Reduced Exposure to Harmful Substances:** Beyond food, adopting organic practices in cleaning and home products reduces exposure to toxins present in many conventional household items. This promotes a healthier indoor environment for you and your family.
- **Connection to Nature:** Creating an organic in-home environment fosters a deeper connection to nature. Studies suggest that exposure to nature positively impacts mental health, reducing stress and promoting overall well-being.

Conclusion:

Choosing organic practices isn't just a choice; it's an investment in your health, a commitment to environmental sustainability, and a step towards overall well-being. By prioritizing organic living within our homes, we not only take care of ourselves but also contribute to a healthier and more sustainable world. As we navigate the journey of harmonizing our living spaces with nature, the benefits ripple beyond our homes, shaping a future where well-being and sustainability walk hand in hand.

Chapter 1: Organic Food in the Home

Organic food refers to agricultural products that are grown, processed, and produced following a set of strict standards designed to promote environmental sustainability, protect animal welfare, and minimize exposure to synthetic chemicals for both consumers and the environment. The production of organic food involves adherence to specific farming practices that prioritize the use of natural methods over synthetic inputs.

Key Principles of Organic Food Production:

1. **No Synthetic Chemicals:**
   - **Pesticides and Herbicides:** Organic farming avoids the use of synthetic pesticides and herbicides. Instead, it relies on natural alternatives, crop rotation, and companion planting to control pests and weeds.
   - **Fertilizers:** Organic agriculture minimizes or eliminates the use of synthetic fertilizers. Nutrient-rich soil is maintained through the application of organic matter, compost, and natural fertilizers.
2. **GMO-Free:**
   - Organic food is produced without the use of genetically modified organisms (GMOs). This ensures that the genetic integrity of crops remains natural, without the introduction of genes from other species.
3. **Animal Welfare:**
   - In the context of organic livestock farming, there are specific standards ensuring the humane treatment of animals. This includes access to outdoor spaces, a balanced and organic diet, and the prohibition of growth hormones or antibiotics.
4. **Sustainable Practices:**
   - Organic farming emphasizes sustainable agricultural practices that maintain soil health and reduce environmental impact. Techniques such as crop rotation, intercropping, and agroforestry contribute to the long-term sustainability of the land.

Certification and Standards:

- Organic food is typically certified by regulatory bodies that verify adherence to organic standards. These standards vary across countries, but they commonly include guidelines related to soil quality, pest and disease management, and the use of synthetic inputs.

Benefits of Choosing Organic Food:

1. **Nutrient Density:**
   - Studies suggest that organic produce may contain higher levels of certain nutrients compared to conventionally grown counterparts.
2. **Reduced Exposure to Chemicals:**
   - Choosing organic helps minimize exposure to synthetic pesticides, herbicides, and fertilizers, potentially reducing the risk of associated health issues.

3. **Environmental Conservation:**
   - Organic farming practices promote biodiversity, reduce soil erosion, and contribute to the conservation of water resources, fostering a more sustainable and eco-friendly agricultural system.

Conclusion:

Choosing organic food goes beyond a dietary choice; it reflects a commitment to health, environmental stewardship, and ethical farming practices. By understanding the principles behind organic food production, consumers can make informed decisions that align with their values and contribute to a more sustainable food system.

Consuming organic food offers a range of benefits, both for individual health and the broader environment. Here's an exploration of the positive impacts associated with choosing organic:

Health Benefits:

1. **Reduced Exposure to Pesticides:**
   - **Organic Farming Practices:** Organic farming avoids the use of synthetic pesticides and herbicides. By choosing organic, consumers minimize their exposure to potentially harmful chemical residues present in conventionally grown produce.
2. **Nutrient Density:**
   - **Higher Nutrient Content:** Some studies suggest that organic fruits and vegetables may have higher levels of certain nutrients compared to their conventionally grown counterparts. This can contribute to a more nutrient-dense diet.
3. **No GMOs:**
   - **Genetically Modified Organisms (GMOs):** Organic food is produced without the use of GMOs. This ensures that consumers are not exposed to genetically modified ingredients, providing an alternative for those who wish to avoid such products.
4. **No Synthetic Hormones or Antibiotics:**
   - **Organic Livestock:** In organic livestock farming, animals are raised without the use of synthetic hormones or antibiotics. Choosing organic meat and dairy products reduces the intake of these substances and supports animal welfare.

Environmental Benefits:

1. **Promotes Soil Health:**
   - **Natural Soil Fertility:** Organic farming practices prioritize the use of natural fertilizers and compost, contributing to soil fertility and structure. This helps maintain the long-term health of the soil.
2. **Reduced Environmental Pollution:**

o **No Synthetic Chemical Runoff:** Organic farming avoids the use of synthetic pesticides and fertilizers that can contribute to chemical runoff, preventing water pollution and protecting aquatic ecosystems.

3. **Biodiversity Conservation:**
   o **Supports Biodiversity:** Organic farms often incorporate practices that support biodiversity, such as maintaining hedgerows, using crop rotation, and avoiding monoculture. This promotes a healthier ecosystem on and around the farm.

4. **Water Conservation:**
   o **Efficient Water Use:** Organic farming typically requires less water than conventional farming. This can be particularly beneficial in regions facing water scarcity, contributing to more sustainable water management practices.

Reduced Carbon Footprint:

- **Carbon Sequestration:** Organic farming practices, such as cover cropping and reduced tillage, contribute to carbon sequestration in the soil. This helps mitigate climate change by reducing the overall carbon footprint of agriculture.

Conclusion:

Choosing organic food is a holistic decision that not only prioritizes personal health but also aligns with environmentally sustainable practices. By supporting organic farming, consumers contribute to a food system that values soil health, biodiversity, and reduced environmental impact, creating a healthier and more sustainable future for individuals and the planet.

The Significance of Locally Sourced and Seasonal Organic Produce: A Culinary and Environmental Journey

In the realm of organic living, the choices we make about the food we consume carry profound implications for our health, the environment, and the communities around us. One crucial aspect of this journey is the emphasis on choosing locally sourced and seasonal organic produce—a practice that extends beyond mere culinary preferences to become a sustainable and conscientious way of nourishing ourselves and the planet.

**1. Culinary Excellence:

- **Freshness and Flavor:** Locally sourced and seasonal produce is harvested at its peak, ensuring optimal freshness and flavor. The proximity of the source means that the time from harvest to your table is minimized, preserving the nutritional value and enhancing taste.
- **Diverse Culinary Experiences:** Embracing seasonal produce introduces a dynamic and diverse array of fruits, vegetables, and herbs to your kitchen. Each season offers a unique palette, inspiring creativity and enriching your culinary experiences.

**2. Health and Nutrition:

- **Nutrient Density:** Locally sourced and seasonal produce often boasts higher nutrient content compared to items that have traveled long distances. The shorter time from farm to table means fewer opportunities for nutrient degradation.
- **Adaptation to Seasonal Needs:** Nature provides what our bodies need at different times of the year. Seasonal eating aligns with our biological needs, offering fruits and vegetables that naturally support our health in different seasons.

**3. Environmental Stewardship:

- **Reduced Carbon Footprint:** Choosing local produce reduces the carbon footprint associated with transportation. By supporting local farmers, we contribute to a more sustainable food system and lower greenhouse gas emissions.
- **Preservation of Biodiversity:** Seasonal eating encourages the cultivation of a variety of crops throughout the year. This diversity is essential for maintaining biodiversity, promoting soil health, and preventing monoculture practices that can lead to environmental degradation.

**4. Community Support:

- **Local Economies:** Purchasing locally sourced produce supports local farmers and economies. This fosters community resilience and helps small-scale farmers thrive, contributing to the vibrancy of local food systems.
- **Connection to Producers:** Buying directly from local producers allows for a more intimate connection between consumers and farmers. This transparency builds trust, and consumers can inquire about farming practices, fostering a deeper understanding of where their food comes from.

**5. Adaptation to Natural Cycles:

- **Harmony with Nature:** Seasonal eating encourages us to reconnect with the natural cycles of the environment. It teaches us patience and appreciation for the unique offerings each season brings, fostering a sense of harmony with the changing world around us.

Conclusion:

Choosing locally sourced and seasonal organic produce is a conscious decision that transcends the act of eating; it is a transformative practice with far-reaching impacts. From the vibrant flavors in your meals to the positive environmental and community contributions, this culinary journey is a celebration of health, sustainability, and harmonious coexistence with the seasons. By making these choices, we not only nourish our bodies but also contribute to a more resilient, sustainable, and interconnected world.

The Dual Impact of Locally Sourced and Seasonal Organic Produce on Health and the Environment

Choosing locally sourced and seasonal organic produce is a powerful decision that resonates on two crucial fronts: individual health and the well-being of the environment. This conscious approach to food consumption not only enriches our well-being but also contributes to a more sustainable and resilient ecosystem.

**1. Health Impact:

- **Nutrient-Rich Eating:** Locally sourced and seasonal produce is harvested at its peak, ensuring maximum nutrient density. Consuming these fresh and unprocessed foods provides our bodies with essential vitamins, minerals, and antioxidants, supporting overall health and vitality.
- **Adaptation to Seasonal Needs:** Seasonal eating aligns with the natural cycles of the environment and our bodies. Fruits and vegetables that flourish in different seasons often contain nutrients that are beneficial for our health during those specific times, promoting a holistic and adaptive approach to nutrition.
- **Reduced Exposure to Harmful Substances:** By choosing local and organic produce, we minimize exposure to harmful pesticides, herbicides, and synthetic fertilizers commonly used in conventional agriculture. This reduction in chemical exposure has positive implications for long-term health.

**2. Environmental Impact:

- **Reduced Carbon Footprint:** Locally sourced produce travels shorter distances from farm to plate, significantly reducing the carbon footprint associated with transportation. This supports a more sustainable and eco-friendly food system by lowering greenhouse gas emissions.
- **Preservation of Biodiversity:** Seasonal eating encourages the cultivation of a diverse range of crops throughout the year. This diversity is crucial for preserving biodiversity, as it prevents monoculture practices that can lead to soil degradation, loss of habitat, and a decline in species diversity.
- **Conservation of Resources:** Local farmers are more likely to employ sustainable agricultural practices, including efficient water use, responsible soil management, and minimal use of synthetic inputs. These practices contribute to the conservation of natural resources and protect ecosystems.
- **Support for Local Economies:** Choosing local produce supports small-scale farmers and local economies. This creates a more resilient and self-sustaining food system, reducing dependency on large-scale industrial agriculture and promoting community well-being.

**3. Culinary and Cultural Impact:

- **Diverse and Flavorful Meals:** Seasonal eating introduces a dynamic array of fruits, vegetables, and herbs to our culinary repertoire, leading to diverse and flavorful meals.

This not only enhances our dining experiences but also encourages creativity in the kitchen.

- **Cultural Connection:** Engaging in seasonal and local eating fosters a deeper connection to the cultural and agricultural heritage of a region. It encourages an appreciation for the unique flavors and traditions associated with each season, enriching our cultural identity.

Conclusion:

The impact of choosing locally sourced and seasonal organic produce extends beyond individual health to encompass the broader health of our planet. By making informed and conscious decisions about the food we consume, we become active participants in creating a more sustainable, resilient, and interconnected food system—one that nurtures both our bodies and the environment we call home.

Scenarios to illustrate how individuals or families successfully integrate organic food practices into their homes.

1. **The Johnson Family: Cultivating an Organic Haven**
   - The Johnson family, living in a suburban neighborhood, transformed their backyard into a thriving organic garden. Emily, the mother, passionately embraced organic gardening principles, incorporating composting and companion planting. The family now enjoys a bountiful harvest of fresh vegetables and herbs throughout the year. The children actively participate in caring for the garden, learning valuable lessons about sustainable living and the importance of knowing where their food comes from.
2. **Eco-Enthusiast Entrepreneur: Sarah's Organic Journey**
   - Sarah, a young entrepreneur, decided to align her personal values with her business venture. She opened an organic cafe in her community, sourcing locally and seasonally for her menu. The cafe quickly became a hub for health-conscious individuals seeking organic, nutrient-rich meals. Sarah's commitment to supporting local farmers not only contributed to the success of her business but also inspired others in the community to explore organic food options.
3. **Urban Homesteaders: The Martinez Family**
   - The Martinez family, living in a small apartment in the city, embraced urban homesteading to integrate organic practices into their daily lives. They started with a small balcony garden, growing herbs and vegetables in containers. To supplement their produce, they joined a local community-supported agriculture (CSA) program. This allowed them to receive a weekly supply of fresh, organic produce directly from local farms. The Martinez family's journey showcases that even in urban settings, it's possible to prioritize organic living.
4. **The Wellness Advocate: Mark's Organic Transformation**
   - Mark, a health-conscious individual with a history of dietary challenges, decided to overhaul his eating habits. He transitioned to a diet centered around organic,

whole foods. Mark's health significantly improved, and he decided to share his journey on social media. His posts about the benefits of organic living, along with practical tips for sourcing organic produce, garnered a large following. Mark's advocacy not only transformed his own life but also inspired others to make healthier and more sustainable food choices.

These stories illustrate the diverse ways in which individuals and families can successfully integrate organic food practices into their homes. Whether through gardening, entrepreneurship, urban homesteading, or personal wellness journeys, these examples highlight the positive impact of embracing organic living.

Chapter 2: Organic Cleaning and Household Products

The Concept of Organic, Eco-Friendly Cleaning Products: A Greener Approach to Clean Living

In recent years, there has been a growing awareness of the impact that traditional cleaning products can have on both human health and the environment. This awareness has given rise to the concept of using organic, eco-friendly cleaning products—a transformative shift toward a greener and more sustainable approach to keeping our homes clean.

**1. Organic Ingredients:

- **Plant-Based Ingredients:** Organic cleaning products are crafted from plant-based ingredients, often derived from renewable resources. These ingredients include extracts from fruits, vegetables, and essential oils, harnessing the power of nature to clean effectively.
- **Avoidance of Harmful Chemicals:** Unlike conventional cleaning products that may contain harsh chemicals, organic alternatives prioritize the exclusion of synthetic fragrances, phosphates, chlorine, and other potentially harmful substances. This focus on natural ingredients reduces the risk of exposure to toxins during cleaning activities.

**2. Eco-Friendly Manufacturing:

- **Sustainable Production Practices:** Manufacturers of organic cleaning products often adhere to sustainable and eco-friendly production practices. This includes using environmentally responsible packaging, minimizing waste, and reducing energy consumption during the manufacturing process.
- **Biodegradability:** Many organic cleaning products are designed to be biodegradable, meaning that they break down into harmless compounds over time. This contrasts with some traditional cleaning products that may contain non-biodegradable ingredients, contributing to environmental pollution.

**3. Safe for Human Health:

- **Reduced Indoor Air Pollution:** Organic cleaning products are generally less likely to release volatile organic compounds (VOCs) into the air. This reduces indoor air pollution, creating a healthier living environment for inhabitants.
- **Allergen-Friendly:** Individuals with allergies or sensitivities may find organic cleaning products to be a gentler option. The absence of synthetic fragrances and harsh chemicals reduces the likelihood of triggering allergic reactions or respiratory issues.

**4. Effective Cleaning Power:

- **Proven Efficacy:** Organic cleaning products have evolved to match, and in some cases surpass, the cleaning power of traditional counterparts. Innovations in formulation and technology have led to the development of effective organic cleaning solutions that can tackle various household cleaning tasks.
- **Multi-Purpose Formulas:** Many organic cleaning products are designed to be multi-purpose, reducing the need for multiple specialized cleaners. This not only simplifies cleaning routines but also minimizes the variety of products entering the home.

**5. Consumer Awareness and Choices:

- **Informed Consumer Choices:** The rise of organic cleaning products reflects a broader shift in consumer awareness. Individuals are increasingly making informed choices, opting for products that align with their values of health, sustainability, and environmental responsibility.
- **Support for Ethical Brands:** The demand for organic, eco-friendly cleaning products has spurred the growth of ethical brands committed to providing high-quality, sustainable alternatives. Supporting these brands contributes to a more sustainable marketplace.

Conclusion:

The concept of using organic, eco-friendly cleaning products is rooted in the recognition that the choices we make in our homes can have far-reaching consequences for both our well-being and the planet. By embracing these products, individuals contribute to a cleaner, healthier living environment while actively participating in the larger movement toward sustainable and mindful consumption.

Unveiling the Hidden Dangers: The Potential Hazards of Conventional Cleaning Products

While conventional cleaning products have become essential tools in maintaining cleanliness and hygiene, it's crucial to be aware of the potential dangers associated with their use. Many conventional cleaners contain a cocktail of chemicals that, when released into our homes and the environment, can pose risks to both human health and the ecosystem. Understanding these potential dangers is a vital step toward making informed choices for a safer and more sustainable living environment.

**1. Exposure to Harmful Chemicals:

- **Volatile Organic Compounds (VOCs):** Many conventional cleaning products contain VOCs, which can contribute to indoor air pollution. These compounds, released during use, can lead to respiratory issues, headaches, and other health concerns.
- **Phthalates and Fragrance Chemicals:** Some cleaning products include phthalates and synthetic fragrances. Phthalates, known endocrine disruptors, may interfere with hormonal balance, while fragrance chemicals can trigger allergic reactions and respiratory problems.

**2. Health Risks for Users:

- **Respiratory Issues:** The inhalation of fumes from conventional cleaning products can lead to respiratory problems, especially for individuals with asthma or other pre-existing conditions.
- **Skin Irritation:** Direct contact with certain cleaning chemicals may cause skin irritation or allergic reactions, particularly for those with sensitive skin.
- **Potential Carcinogens:** Some conventional cleaners may contain ingredients classified as potential carcinogens or substances that have not undergone sufficient long-term safety testing.

**3. Environmental Impact:

- **Water Pollution:** The chemicals in cleaning products, when washed down drains, can contribute to water pollution. This may harm aquatic ecosystems and affect the quality of water sources.
- **Soil Contamination:** Residues from cleaning products can end up in the soil, potentially leading to soil contamination and negatively impacting plant and microbial life.

**4. Hazardous Waste Concerns:

- **Disposal Challenges:** Improper disposal of conventional cleaning products, especially those labeled as hazardous waste, poses challenges for waste management systems and can contribute to environmental pollution.

**5. Impact on Indoor Environment:

- **Endocrine Disruption:** Certain chemicals found in cleaning products, such as phthalates and triclosan, have been associated with endocrine disruption. This can have long-term effects on hormonal balance and overall health.
- **Children and Vulnerable Populations:** Children, pregnant individuals, and those with compromised immune systems may be more susceptible to the adverse effects of exposure to cleaning product chemicals.

**6. Contribution to Antibiotic Resistance:

- **Antibacterial Agents:** The use of antibacterial agents, like triclosan, in cleaning products, may contribute to antibiotic resistance, diminishing the effectiveness of these drugs in fighting bacterial infections.

Conclusion:

Awareness of the potential dangers associated with conventional cleaning products underscores the need for a cautious and informed approach to household cleaning. As consumers become more conscious of the impact of their choices, the demand for safer, eco-friendly alternatives is on the rise. Transitioning to organic and environmentally friendly cleaning products is not only a step toward safeguarding personal health but also a contribution to a cleaner, healthier planet.

DIY Organic Cleaning Recipes

1. All-Purpose Cleaner:

- **Ingredients:**
    - 1 cup distilled white vinegar
    - 1 cup water
    - 1 tablespoon baking soda
    - 10-15 drops of essential oil (e.g., tea tree, lavender, lemon for additional fragrance and antibacterial properties)
- **Instructions:**
    1. In a mixing bowl, combine the distilled white vinegar and water.
    2. Slowly add the baking soda to the mixture. Be cautious, as it may produce some fizz.
    3. Once the fizzing subsides, stir the mixture until the baking soda is dissolved.
    4. Add your chosen essential oil and stir again.
    5. Pour the mixture into a spray bottle and shake well before each use.
- **Usage:**
    - Use this all-purpose cleaner on countertops, surfaces, glass, and other non-porous surfaces.

2. Citrus Vinegar Cleaner:

- **Ingredients:**
    - Citrus peels (e.g., orange, lemon, grapefruit)
    - White vinegar
    - A large glass jar with a lid
- **Instructions:**
    1. Fill the glass jar with citrus peels.
    2. Pour white vinegar over the peels until they are fully submerged.
    3. Seal the jar with the lid and let it sit in a cool, dark place for about 2 weeks.
    4. Strain the citrus-infused vinegar into a spray bottle.
- **Usage:**
    - This citrus-infused vinegar cleaner is excellent for cutting through grease and grime. Use it on surfaces like kitchen counters and stovetops.

3. Baking Soda Scrub:

- **Ingredients:**
    - Baking soda
    - Water
- **Instructions:**
    1. In a small bowl, mix baking soda with enough water to create a paste.
    2. Adjust the consistency as needed.
- **Usage:**

o   Use the baking soda scrub to clean sinks, tubs, and surfaces that require a gentle abrasive action. Apply the paste, scrub, and rinse.

**4. Window and Glass Cleaner:

- **Ingredients:**
    - o   1 cup distilled white vinegar
    - o   1 cup water
- **Instructions:**
    1. Mix equal parts distilled white vinegar and water in a spray bottle.
- **Usage:**
    - o   Spray this solution on windows and glass surfaces, and wipe clean with a lint-free cloth or newspaper.

**5. Disinfectant Spray:

- **Ingredients:**
    - o   1 cup rubbing alcohol (at least 60% alcohol content)
    - o   1 cup water
    - o   10 drops tea tree oil
    - o   10 drops lavender oil (or your preferred essential oil)
- **Instructions:**
    1. Combine rubbing alcohol and water in a spray bottle.
    2. Add the tea tree oil and lavender oil.
    3. Shake well to mix the ingredients thoroughly.
- **Usage:**
    - o   Use this disinfectant spray on frequently-touched surfaces such as doorknobs, light switches, and countertops.

These DIY organic cleaning solutions are versatile, effective, and free from harsh chemicals, offering a safe and sustainable alternative to conventional cleaners. Adjust the quantities based on your needs and preferences.

The effectiveness of DIY organic cleaning alternatives depends on the specific cleaning task and the ingredients used. While these alternatives may not have the same industrial strength as some commercial cleaners, they are often highly effective for everyday cleaning needs. Here's a discussion of the effectiveness of the mentioned alternatives:

**1. All-Purpose Cleaner:

- **Effectiveness:** The all-purpose cleaner made with vinegar, water, baking soda, and essential oils is excellent for general cleaning tasks. Vinegar has natural antibacterial properties, and baking soda provides mild abrasion for scrubbing. Essential oils add a pleasant scent and additional antibacterial properties.

**2. Citrus Vinegar Cleaner:

- **Effectiveness:** The citrus-infused vinegar cleaner is great for cutting through grease and providing a fresh scent. The natural acidity of citrus helps dissolve grime, while the vinegar acts as a disinfectant.

**3. Baking Soda Scrub:

- **Effectiveness:** Baking soda is an effective abrasive agent that can tackle a variety of cleaning tasks without scratching surfaces. It's particularly useful for removing stains, mildew, and soap scum.

**4. Window and Glass Cleaner:

- **Effectiveness:** The vinegar and water mixture makes an effective glass cleaner. Vinegar helps to break down and dissolve residues on glass surfaces, leaving them streak-free when wiped with a lint-free cloth or newspaper.

**5. Disinfectant Spray:

- **Effectiveness:** The disinfectant spray with rubbing alcohol and essential oils is effective for disinfecting surfaces. Rubbing alcohol is a powerful disinfectant, and tea tree oil adds antimicrobial properties. However, it's important to note that the effectiveness may vary based on the alcohol content of the rubbing alcohol.

Considerations:

- **Surface Compatibility:** While these alternatives work well on various surfaces, it's important to consider the material of the surface being cleaned. For example, vinegar may not be suitable for certain types of stone surfaces.
- **Personal Preferences:** The effectiveness of these alternatives can also be influenced by personal preferences. Some individuals may find the scent of vinegar strong, while others appreciate the natural, clean aroma.
- **Consistency and Frequency:** Consistency in using these alternatives and regular cleaning routines contribute to their overall effectiveness. For tougher stains or heavily soiled areas, you may need to repeat the cleaning process or use more concentrated solutions.

Conclusion:

DIY organic cleaning alternatives can be highly effective for maintaining a clean and healthy home. They are particularly suitable for routine cleaning tasks and are often safer for both your health and the environment. However, for specific cleaning challenges or heavy-duty tasks, it's advisable to assess the situation and, if needed, use additional cleaning methods. Overall, the effectiveness of these alternatives makes them valuable tools for those seeking a greener and more sustainable approach to household cleaning.

While I can't provide specific real-life examples due to privacy concerns, I can share common scenarios inspired by households that have adopted organic cleaning practices. These examples highlight the motivations, challenges, and benefits that individuals and families may experience when transitioning to organic cleaning in their homes.

**1. The Green Living Enthusiasts: The Smith Family

- **Motivation:** The Smith family, passionate about sustainability and eco-friendly living, decided to overhaul their cleaning routine to align with their values. Concerned about the impact of traditional cleaning products on the environment and their health, they embraced a variety of DIY organic cleaning solutions.
- **Challenges:** Initially, the family faced resistance from family members who were accustomed to the familiar scents of conventional cleaners. Overcoming this resistance involved experimenting with different essential oil combinations to find pleasant and acceptable fragrances.
- **Benefits:** The Smith family experienced a noticeable improvement in indoor air quality and a reduction in allergy symptoms. Additionally, their children actively participated in creating the homemade cleaners, turning the cleaning process into a family bonding activity.

**2. The Health-Conscious Home: Sarah's Journey

- **Motivation:** Sarah, a health-conscious individual with sensitivities to synthetic fragrances and harsh chemicals, sought alternatives to traditional cleaning products. Her journey toward organic cleaning was driven by a desire to create a healthier home environment.
- **Challenges:** Sarah initially struggled to find effective alternatives that met her cleanliness standards. Through research and experimentation, she discovered the power of simple solutions like vinegar, baking soda, and essential oils.
- **Benefits:** Switching to organic cleaning products significantly reduced the skin irritation and respiratory issues Sarah previously experienced. Her journey inspired her to share her knowledge with friends and family, creating a ripple effect of awareness.

**3. Urban Homesteaders: The Martinez Apartment

- **Motivation:** Living in a small urban apartment, the Martinez family wanted to create a sustainable and organic lifestyle despite limited space. They started by growing some herbs on their balcony and gradually incorporated homemade cleaning solutions into their routine.
- **Challenges:** Space constraints forced the family to be creative with their gardening efforts, utilizing vertical space for herbs and compact plants. Adjusting to a new cleaning routine required patience as they experimented with different formulations.
- **Benefits:** The Martinez family enjoyed the dual benefits of fresh herbs for cooking and organic cleaning solutions that were safe for their small living space. Their journey showcased that organic living is achievable even in urban settings.

**4. The Minimalist Approach: Mark's Story

- **Motivation:** Mark, a minimalist seeking to simplify his lifestyle, decided to declutter not just physical possessions but also the cleaning products under his sink. He replaced a variety of commercial cleaners with a few key organic alternatives.
- **Challenges:** Initially, Mark worried that simplifying his cleaning routine might compromise cleanliness. However, he found that a few versatile organic solutions were effective for most tasks.
- **Benefits:** Mark's minimalist approach not only reduced clutter but also minimized his environmental impact. He appreciated the ease of cleaning with fewer products, emphasizing the principle of "less is more."

These examples illustrate that households adopt organic cleaning practices for various reasons, including health concerns, environmental consciousness, and a desire for a simpler lifestyle. Despite initial challenges, many individuals and families find the transition to organic cleaning to be rewarding, contributing to a healthier home and a more sustainable way of living.

Chapter 3: Sustainable Living Practices

Home energy efficiency using organic methods involves adopting practices and making choices that are environmentally friendly, sustainable, and prioritize natural resources. Here are several ways to make your home more energy-efficient using organic methods:

**1. Energy-Efficient Lighting:

- **Organic Approach:** opt for energy-efficient lighting solutions such as LED (light-emitting diode) or CFL (compact fluorescent lamp) bulbs. These bulbs are more energy-efficient and have a longer lifespan compared to traditional incandescent bulbs.
- **Benefits:** LED and CFL bulbs consume less energy, produce less heat, and contain fewer hazardous materials. They are also recyclable, contributing to a more sustainable lighting solution.

**2. Natural Insulation Materials:

- **Organic Approach:** Choose natural and organic insulation materials, such as wool, cotton, or recycled denim, instead of synthetic alternatives. These materials are renewable, biodegradable, and often have lower environmental impact.
- **Benefits:** Natural insulation provides effective thermal resistance, reducing the need for excessive heating or cooling. Additionally, these materials are often less harmful to human health during installation and use.

**3. Strategic Landscaping:

- **Organic Approach:** Plant trees strategically around your home to provide shade in the summer and allow sunlight in during the winter. Consider using native plants that require less water and maintenance.
- **Benefits:** Well-placed trees and shrubs act as natural insulation, reducing the need for artificial heating and cooling. They also contribute to biodiversity and create a more comfortable outdoor environment.

**4. Organic Energy Sources:

- **Organic Approach:** Invest in renewable energy sources, such as solar panels or wind turbines. These systems generate electricity using natural elements and can often be integrated into the architecture of the home.
- **Benefits:** Utilizing solar or wind energy reduces dependence on non-renewable resources and lowers your carbon footprint. It also allows homeowners to generate their own clean energy.

**5. Energy-Efficient Appliances:

- **Organic Approach:** Choose appliances with high energy efficiency ratings. Look for products that are certified by energy efficiency labels, such as ENERGY STAR.
- **Benefits:** Energy-efficient appliances consume less electricity, leading to reduced energy bills and a lower environmental impact. They often use advanced technologies to optimize performance while minimizing energy consumption.

**6. Natural Ventilation:

- **Organic Approach:** Design your home to maximize natural ventilation. Use windows, skylights, and cross-ventilation to allow fresh air to circulate and cool the home without relying on air conditioning.
- **Benefits:** Natural ventilation promotes a healthier indoor environment by reducing the buildup of indoor pollutants. It also minimizes the need for mechanical cooling systems, saving energy.

**7. Energy-Efficient Windows:

- **Organic Approach:** Install energy-efficient windows with proper insulation. Consider double-glazed windows or those with low-emissivity coatings to reduce heat transfer.
- **Benefits:** Energy-efficient windows contribute to better insulation, maintaining a comfortable indoor temperature without excessive reliance on heating or cooling systems. They also enhance natural light and reduce the need for artificial lighting during the day.

**8. Water Conservation:

- **Organic Approach:** Implement water-efficient practices, such as using rainwater harvesting systems, installing low-flow faucets and showerheads, and choosing drought-resistant landscaping.
- **Benefits:** Water-efficient practices contribute to overall sustainability and can reduce the energy required for water heating. Additionally, they support responsible water use in regions facing water scarcity.

**9. Eco-Friendly Building Materials:

- **Organic Approach:** Choose eco-friendly, organic building materials for construction or renovation. Consider materials like bamboo, reclaimed wood, or recycled metal.
- **Benefits:** Eco-friendly building materials often have lower environmental impacts in terms of production and transportation. They contribute to a healthier indoor environment by reducing the off-gassing of harmful chemicals.

**10. Smart Home Technology:

- **Organic Approach:** Utilize smart home technology to optimize energy use. Smart thermostats, lighting controls, and energy-monitoring systems can help you manage energy consumption more efficiently.

- **Benefits:** Smart home technology allows for precise control over energy usage, helping to reduce waste and optimize efficiency. It also enhances convenience and comfort.

Conclusion:

Improving home energy efficiency using organic methods involves a holistic approach that considers the impact of every choice on the environment. By incorporating sustainable practices, utilizing renewable energy sources, and choosing organic materials, homeowners can create energy-efficient homes that promote a healthier living environment and contribute to a more sustainable future.

Adopting organic methods to make a home more energy-efficient brings a myriad of benefits, impacting both the environment and the household positively. Here's a comprehensive overview of the advantages:

Benefits for the Environment:

1. **Reduced Carbon Footprint:**
   - *How:* The use of renewable energy sources like solar panels and wind turbines reduces reliance on non-renewable resources, lowering carbon emissions.
   - *Impact:* Mitigating climate change by minimizing the carbon footprint associated with energy consumption.
2. **Conservation of Natural Resources:**
   - *How:* Choosing natural and organic materials, as well as implementing energy-efficient practices, reduces the demand for resource-intensive manufacturing processes.
   - *Impact:* Preserving ecosystems, reducing deforestation, and conserving water resources.
3. **Biodiversity Conservation:**
   - *How:* Sustainable landscaping practices, including planting native vegetation, contribute to biodiversity by providing habitats for local flora and fauna.
   - *Impact:* Supporting the health of ecosystems and fostering a more balanced and resilient natural environment.
4. **Reduced Pollution:**
   - *How:* Opting for eco-friendly appliances, materials, and cleaning solutions minimizes the release of harmful pollutants into the air and water.
   - *Impact:* Improving air and water quality, reducing pollution-related health issues, and supporting a cleaner environment.
5. **Mitigation of Habitat Destruction:**
   - *How:* Sustainable construction practices and landscaping help minimize habitat destruction associated with urban development.
   - *Impact:* Preserving natural habitats and minimizing the impact on wildlife populations.
6. **Promotion of Circular Economy:**
   - *How:* Choosing organic and recycled materials supports a circular economy by reducing waste and encouraging the reuse of resources.

o   *Impact:* Contributing to a more sustainable and less wasteful economic model.

Benefits for the Household:

1. **Cost Savings:**
   - o   *How:* Energy-efficient appliances, lighting, and insulation reduce energy consumption, leading to lower utility bills.
   - o   *Impact:* Significant cost savings over time, contributing to long-term financial well-being.
2. **Improved Indoor Air Quality:**
   - o   *How:* Using natural and organic materials, as well as implementing proper ventilation strategies, enhances indoor air quality.
   - o   *Impact:* Reducing the risk of respiratory issues, allergies, and other health concerns associated with poor indoor air quality.
3. **Increased Comfort and Well-being:**
   - o   *How:* Proper insulation, natural lighting, and smart home technologies contribute to a more comfortable living environment.
   - o   *Impact:* Enhancing the overall well-being and comfort of occupants, fostering a positive home environment.
4. **Long-Term Durability:**
   - o   *How:* Choosing high-quality, organic building materials often results in more durable and resilient structures.
   - o   *Impact:* Reducing the need for frequent repairs and replacements, leading to long-term cost savings and less environmental impact.
5. **Energy Independence:**
   - o   *How:* Installing renewable energy sources, like solar panels, provides a degree of energy independence and resilience against power outages.
   - o   *Impact:* Ensuring a more reliable energy supply and potentially reducing dependence on external energy sources.
6. **Contribution to Sustainable Practices:**
   - o   *How:* Adopting organic and eco-friendly practices sets an example for others in the community and contributes to a broader cultural shift towards sustainability.
   - o   *Impact:* Encouraging a more sustainable lifestyle and influencing positive changes in the community.

Conclusion:

The benefits of adopting organic methods for energy efficiency extend far beyond the household, positively impacting the environment and contributing to a more sustainable and resilient future. From reducing environmental impact to improving overall well-being, these practices showcase the interconnectedness of individual choices with broader environmental and societal outcomes.

Reducing waste and increasing recycling in the home is an effective way to minimize environmental impact and contribute to a more sustainable lifestyle. Here are strategies to help achieve this goal:

1. Adopt a Zero-Waste Mindset:

- **Approach:** Embrace a zero-waste mindset by being mindful of the products you purchase and the waste you generate.
- **Implementation:**
  - Prioritize reusable items over disposable ones (e.g., cloth bags, water bottles, and containers).
  - Choose products with minimal or eco-friendly packaging.

2. Set Up a Home Recycling Station:

- **Approach:** Create a designated space in your home for sorting and storing recyclables.
- **Implementation:**
  - Label bins or containers for different types of recyclables (e.g., paper, plastic, glass, metal).
  - Educate family members on what can and cannot be recycled.

3. Composting Organic Waste:

- **Approach:** Composting organic waste reduces the amount of food and yard waste sent to landfills.
- **Implementation:**
  - Set up a composting bin for kitchen scraps like fruit and vegetable peels.
  - Compost yard waste like leaves and grass clippings.

4. Mindful Shopping:

- **Approach:** Make informed and sustainable choices while shopping to reduce packaging waste.
- **Implementation:**
  - Buy in bulk to minimize packaging.
  - Choose products with minimal or recyclable packaging.

5. Repair and Reuse:

- **Approach:** Extend the life of products by repairing and reusing them.
- **Implementation:**
  - Mend clothing and household items instead of discarding them.
  - Donate or sell items you no longer need.

6. Educate Household Members:

- **Approach:** Foster a culture of waste reduction by educating family members.
- **Implementation:**
  - Discuss the importance of reducing waste and recycling with everyone in the household.

o   Encourage responsible waste management habits.

**7. Choose Recyclable and Recycled Products:

- **Approach:** Opt for products that are recyclable or made from recycled materials.
- **Implementation:**
    o   Look for the recycling symbol on packaging.
    o   Support brands committed to using recycled materials.

**8. E-Waste Recycling:

- **Approach:** Properly dispose of electronic waste (e-waste) through recycling programs.
- **Implementation:**
    o   Find local e-waste recycling centers or participate in e-waste collection events.
    o   Donate or sell working electronics.

**9. Upcycling Projects:

- **Approach:** Get creative by upcycling items into new and useful products.
- **Implementation:**
    o   Turn old jars into storage containers.
    o   Repurpose furniture or clothing items.

**10. Monitor and Reduce Energy Consumption:

- **Approach:** Reduce the environmental impact associated with energy use.
- **Implementation:**
    o   Switch to energy-efficient appliances.
    o   Turn off lights and electronics when not in use.

**11. Participate in Community Recycling Programs:

- **Approach:** Engage with local recycling initiatives and programs.
- **Implementation:**
    o   Check for community recycling events or drop-off locations.
    o   Join or support local environmental groups.

**12. Support Extended Producer Responsibility (EPR):

- **Approach:** Advocate for responsible product lifecycle management.
- **Implementation:**
    o   Support brands with extended producer responsibility, encouraging them to take responsibility for the disposal and recycling of their products.

Conclusion:

Implementing these strategies for waste reduction and increased recycling in the home not only contributes to a more sustainable lifestyle but also sets a positive example for others in the community. By adopting these practices, individuals can make a significant impact on reducing waste and fostering a more environmentally conscious living environment.

Implementing waste reduction and recycling practices in the home has a substantial positive impact on the environment. These practices contribute to several environmental benefits, promoting sustainability and minimizing the negative effects of excessive waste generation. Here's a discussion of the environmental impact of these practices:

**1. Reduction of Landfill Waste:

- **Impact:** By adopting a zero-waste mindset, prioritizing reusable items, and minimizing packaging, households contribute to a significant reduction in the amount of waste sent to landfills.
- **Benefit:** Reducing landfill waste helps prevent soil contamination, minimizes greenhouse gas emissions from decomposing waste, and conserves valuable land resources.

**2. Conservation of Natural Resources:

- **Impact:** Mindful shopping, choosing products with minimal packaging, and opting for recycled materials contribute to the conservation of natural resources.
- **Benefit:** Reduced demand for raw materials and resources helps protect ecosystems, prevent habitat destruction, and conserve biodiversity.

**3. Energy Savings through Recycling:

- **Impact:** Recycling materials like paper, glass, and metal consumes less energy than producing new materials from virgin resources.
- **Benefit:** Lower energy consumption in the recycling process leads to reduced greenhouse gas emissions and a smaller ecological footprint.

**4. Mitigation of Ocean Pollution:

- **Impact:** Proper disposal and recycling of plastic waste prevent the accumulation of plastic debris in oceans and waterways.
- **Benefit:** Reducing ocean pollution protects marine life, prevents harm to ecosystems, and supports the overall health of aquatic environments.

**5. Improved Soil Quality:

- **Impact:** Composting organic waste helps create nutrient-rich compost, improving soil quality.
- **Benefit:** Healthy soil supports plant growth, enhances agricultural productivity, and reduces the need for synthetic fertilizers, which can have environmental impacts.

**6. Reduced Greenhouse Gas Emissions:

- **Impact:** Waste reduction practices, such as composting and recycling, contribute to a reduction in overall greenhouse gas emissions.
- **Benefit:** Lower greenhouse gas emissions help mitigate climate change and its associated impacts, including rising temperatures, extreme weather events, and disruptions to ecosystems.

**7. Resource-Efficient Manufacturing:

- **Impact:** Choosing products made from recycled materials encourages resource-efficient manufacturing processes.
- **Benefit:** Resource-efficient manufacturing conserves energy and raw materials, leading to a smaller environmental footprint associated with the production of goods.

**8. Protection of Wildlife:

- **Impact:** Reducing waste, particularly plastic waste, helps protect wildlife from ingestion and entanglement.
- **Benefit:** Preserving wildlife habitats and reducing the threat of harm from waste materials support the well-being of diverse ecosystems.

**9. Promotion of Circular Economy:

- **Impact:** Recycling and upcycling practices contribute to the development of a circular economy.
- **Benefit:** A circular economy minimizes waste by promoting the continual use, recycling, and repurposing of materials, reducing the need for constant extraction of new resources.

**10. Positive Environmental Influence:

- **Impact:** Community engagement in recycling programs and waste reduction initiatives creates a positive environmental influence.
- **Benefit:** The cumulative impact of widespread adoption of these practices can lead to significant positive changes, influencing broader environmental consciousness and sustainability.

Conclusion:

The environmental impact of waste reduction and recycling practices in the home is far-reaching, touching on various aspects of ecological sustainability. By embracing these practices, individuals contribute to the protection of ecosystems, the conservation of resources, and the overall well-being of the planet. These collective efforts play a vital role in building a more sustainable and resilient future for the environment and future generations.

Integrating organic principles into home design and construction involves adopting sustainable, environmentally friendly practices that prioritize the use of natural materials, energy efficiency, and overall eco-conscious design. Here are ways in which organic principles can be incorporated into various aspects of home design and construction:

**1. Sustainable Site Selection and Landscaping:

- **Principle:** Choose a site that minimizes environmental impact, considering factors like soil quality, water conservation, and existing ecosystems.
- **Implementation:**
  - Preserve existing vegetation and natural features.
  - Implement water-efficient landscaping with native plants.

**2. Energy-Efficient Design:

- **Principle:** Design homes with a focus on energy efficiency to reduce the environmental footprint.
- **Implementation:**
  - Utilize passive solar design for natural heating and cooling.
  - Optimize the orientation and placement of windows to maximize natural light.
  - Invest in energy-efficient appliances and lighting.

**3. Natural and Renewable Building Materials:

- **Principle:** Prioritize the use of natural, renewable, and eco-friendly building materials.
- **Implementation:**
  - Choose sustainably harvested wood or bamboo for flooring and furniture.
  - Opt for recycled or reclaimed materials for construction.
  - Explore alternatives like rammed earth, adobe, or straw bale construction.

**4. Energy-Efficient Insulation:

- **Principle:** Focus on effective insulation to minimize energy consumption for heating and cooling.
- **Implementation:**
  - Use natural insulation materials like sheep's wool, recycled denim, or cork.
  - Consider advanced insulation techniques, such as straw bale construction or green roofs.

**5. Water Efficiency:

- **Principle:** Implement water-efficient design and technology to reduce water consumption.
- **Implementation:**
  - Install low-flow faucets, showerheads, and dual-flush toilets.
  - Incorporate rainwater harvesting systems for irrigation or household use.

o   Consider greywater systems to reuse water from sinks and showers.

**6. Natural Ventilation and Indoor Air Quality:

- **Principle:** Prioritize natural ventilation and maintain high indoor air quality.
- **Implementation:**
    o   Design spaces with cross-ventilation and operable windows.
    o   Use non-toxic paints, finishes, and adhesives to minimize indoor air pollution.
    o   Include indoor plants to improve air quality.

**7. Renewable Energy Integration:

- **Principle:** Incorporate renewable energy sources to power the home.
- **Implementation:**
    o   Install solar panels or solar water heaters.
    o   Explore wind or geothermal energy options if suitable for the location.

**8. Waste Reduction and Recycling:

- **Principle:** Minimize waste during construction and prioritize recycling.
- **Implementation:**
    o   Choose construction methods that produce less waste.
    o   Recycle or repurpose construction materials.

**9. Durability and Longevity:

- **Principle:** Design and construct homes with durability in mind to reduce the need for frequent repairs and replacements.
- **Implementation:**
    o   Use high-quality, durable materials that withstand the test of time.
    o   Consider modular or prefabricated construction for efficiency and longevity.

**10. Community and Social Sustainability:

- **Principle:** Consider the social impact of home design on the community.
- **Implementation:**
    o   Design spaces that foster community interaction.
    o   Prioritize accessibility and inclusivity in design.

**11. Integrated Technology for Efficiency:

- **Principle:** Utilize smart home technology for energy efficiency and convenience.
- **Implementation:**
    o   Install smart thermostats, lighting controls, and energy-monitoring systems.
    o   Explore home automation for optimizing energy use.

****12. Lifecycle Considerations:**

- **Principle:** Consider the entire lifecycle of materials and design elements.
- **Implementation:**
    - Choose materials that are easy to recycle or biodegradable.
    - Plan for adaptability and potential future renovations.

Conclusion:

Integrating organic principles into home design and construction involves a holistic and mindful approach. By prioritizing sustainability, energy efficiency, and the use of natural materials, individuals can contribute to the creation of homes that not only meet the needs of occupants but also harmonize with the environment and promote a healthier, more eco-conscious way of living.

Using sustainable materials in construction and design is a fundamental aspect of creating environmentally friendly and socially responsible buildings. Sustainable materials are those that have a reduced impact on the environment throughout their lifecycle, from extraction or cultivation to production, use, and disposal. Here are various categories of sustainable materials commonly employed in construction and design:

**1. Wood from Sustainable Sources:

- **Description:** Timber from responsibly managed forests certified by organizations like the Forest Stewardship Council (FSC).
- **Benefits:**
    - Renewable resources.
    - Supports sustainable forestry practices.
    - Carbon sequestration potential.

**2. Bamboo:

- **Description:** A rapidly renewable resource with strength and versatility comparable to hardwood.
- **Benefits:**
    - Fast growth rate.
    - Low environmental impact.
    - Versatile applications in construction.

**3. Recycled and Reclaimed Materials:

- **Description:** Materials salvaged from previous buildings or manufactured from recycled content.
- **Benefits:**
    - Diverts waste from landfills.
    - Reduces the need for virgin materials.
    - Preserves historical or unique elements.

4. Cork:

- **Description:** Harvested from the bark of cork oak trees without causing harm to the tree.
- **Benefits:**
    - Renewable and sustainable.
    - Lightweight and insulating.
    - Resistant to pests and fire.

5. Recycled Metal:

- **Description:** Metal extracted from scrap or post-consumer sources.
- **Benefits:**
    - Reduces energy consumption compared to virgin metal production.
    - Highly durable and recyclable.

6. Rammed Earth:

- **Description:** Construction technique using natural raw materials like earth, chalk, lime, or gravel.
- **Benefits:**
    - Low environmental impact.
    - Excellent thermal mass properties.
    - Aesthetic appeal.

7. Straw Bales:

- **Description:** Bales made from straw, a byproduct of grain harvesting, used in construction.
- **Benefits:**
    - Abundant agricultural byproduct.
    - Good insulation properties.
    - Carbon sequestration potential.

8. Hempcrete:

- **Description:** Mixture of hemp fibers, lime, and water used as a building material.
- **Benefits:**
    - Renewable and fast-growing crop.
    - High insulation properties.
    - Carbon-negative over its lifecycle.

9. Recycled Glass:

- **Description:** Glass cullet from recycled bottles or industrial glass used in construction.
- **Benefits:**
    - Reduces energy consumption in glass production.

- o   Conserves raw materials.
- o   Adds aesthetic diversity.

**10. Linoleum:

- **Description:** Flooring material made from linseed oil, wood flour, cork dust, and other natural materials.
- **Benefits:**
  - o   Biodegradable and recyclable.
  - o   Low environmental impact during production.
  - o   Long lifespan.

**11. Low-VOC and Non-Toxic Paints:

- **Description:** Paints with low or no volatile organic compounds (VOCs) that emit fewer harmful chemicals.
- **Benefits:**
  - o   Improves indoor air quality.
  - o   Reduces the release of harmful pollutants.
  - o   Less impact on human health.

**12. FSC-Certified Plywood:

- **Description:** Plywood made from wood certified by the Forest Stewardship Council.
- **Benefits:**
  - o   Supports sustainable forestry practices.
  - o   Ensures responsible wood sourcing.

**13. Solar Tiles:

- **Description:** Roof tiles with integrated solar cells.
- **Benefits:**
  - o   Generates renewable energy.
  - o   Aesthetic integration into building design.

**14. Recycled Steel:

- **Description:** Steel made from recycled scrap metal.
- **Benefits:**
  - o   Reduces energy use in steel production.
  - o   Highly durable and recyclable.

**15. Sheep's Wool Insulation:

- **Description:** Natural insulation material made from sheep's wool.
- **Benefits:**

- o Renewable and biodegradable.
- o Effective insulation properties.
- o Low environmental impact.

**16. Geopolymer Concrete:

- **Description:** Cement alternative with reduced carbon emissions during production.
- **Benefits:**
    - o Lower carbon footprint compared to traditional concrete.
    - o High durability.

**17. Green Roofs:

- **Description:** Roofs covered with vegetation, soil, and a waterproofing layer.
- **Benefits:**
    - o Improves energy efficiency.
    - o Reduces stormwater runoff.
    - o Enhances biodiversity.

**18. Eco-Friendly Carpets:

- **Description:** Carpets made from natural fibers like wool or recycled materials.
- **Benefits:**
    - o Biodegradable or recyclable.
    - o Reduces dependence on synthetic materials.

**19. Sustainable Concrete Alternatives:

- **Description:** Innovations like ashcrete or recycled concrete reduce the environmental impact of traditional concrete.
- **Benefits:**
    - o Reduces reliance on cement production.
    - o Utilizes waste materials.

**20. Modular Construction:

- **Description:** Buildings constructed with prefabricated modules off-site, reducing waste and energy during construction.
- **Benefits:**
    - o Efficient use of materials.
    - o Faster construction timelines.
    - o Minimizes site disruption.

Conclusion:

The use of sustainable materials in construction and design is crucial for creating environmentally responsible and resilient buildings. By choosing materials that prioritize environmental impact reduction, energy efficiency, and renewable resources, individuals and industries contribute to a more sustainable and regenerative built environment.

These examples showcase a range of approaches, from energy-efficient design to the use of eco-friendly materials and the incorporation of renewable energy sources. Here are a few notable examples:

**1. The Green Building, Louisville, Kentucky:

- **Features:**
    - LEED Platinum certified building.
    - Rooftop garden and green space.
    - Rainwater harvesting system.
    - Energy-efficient design and renewable energy sources.

**2. The Heliotrope, Germany:

- **Features:**
    - Rotating solar-powered house.
    - Designed to maximize solar exposure for energy efficiency.
    - Utilizes natural ventilation and passive solar design.
    - Rainwater harvesting system for irrigation.

**3. Earthships, Various Locations Worldwide:

- **Features:**
    - Sustainable, off-grid homes made from natural and recycled materials.
    - Utilize passive solar design for heating and cooling.
    - Incorporate rainwater harvesting and greywater recycling.
    - Designed to be self-sufficient in terms of energy and water.

**4. The Cottages at Hickory Crossing, Dallas, Texas:

- **Features:**
    - Affordable housing project focused on sustainability.
    - Energy-efficient design and appliances.
    - Rainwater harvesting for irrigation.
    - Community garden for residents.

**5. The Biosphere 2, Arizona:

- **Features:**
    - Sustainable living experiment.
    - Closed ecological system with rainforest, ocean, and agricultural areas.
    - Emphasizes organic farming practices and renewable energy sources.

**6. The ZeroHouse, Colorado:

- **Features:**
    - Net-zero energy home.
    - Utilizes solar panels for electricity.
    - Energy-efficient design and appliances.
    - Rainwater harvesting system.

**7. The Hemp House, Asheville, North Carolina:

- **Features:**
    - Constructed using hempcrete, a sustainable and eco-friendly building material.
    - Energy-efficient design.
    - Utilizes natural and non-toxic materials.

**8. The ZEB Pilot House, Norway:

- **Features:**
    - Zero-emission building.
    - Utilizes solar panels and geothermal energy for electricity.
    - High level of insulation and energy-efficient design.

**9. The Permaculture Research Institute, Australia:

- **Features:**
    - Demonstrates permaculture principles for sustainable living.
    - Incorporates organic gardening and food production.
    - Emphasizes water conservation and recycling.

**10. The S House, Vietnam:

- **Features:**
    - Sustainable design using local and recycled materials.
    - Utilizes natural ventilation and daylighting.
    - Rainwater harvesting system.
    - Emphasizes a connection with nature.

**11. The Green School, Bali:

- **Features:**
    - Sustainable and eco-friendly bamboo architecture.
    - Emphasizes environmental education and permaculture.
    - Utilizes renewable energy sources.

**12. The Green Village, Bali:

- **Features:**
  - o Sustainable bamboo homes and structures.
  - o Emphasizes eco-friendly living and sustainable design.
  - o Utilizes natural ventilation and lighting.

13. The Kalkin House, Vermont:

- **Features:**
  - o Repurposed shipping containers for construction.
  - o Utilizes solar panels for electricity.
  - o Energy-efficient design and materials.

14. The Eco-Village, Findhorn, Scotland:

- **Features:**
  - o Community committed to sustainability and organic living.
  - o Emphasizes renewable energy sources and eco-friendly construction.
  - o Integrates permaculture principles.

15. The Treehouse, Costa Rica:

- **Features:**
  - o Sustainable and eco-friendly treehouse accommodation.
  - o Built with reclaimed materials.
  - o Utilizes rainwater harvesting and solar power.

These examples demonstrate the diverse ways in which sustainable and organic living practices can be integrated into residential design and construction, from energy efficiency and renewable energy sources to the use of eco-friendly materials and organic gardening. Each project reflects a commitment to environmental stewardship and a desire to create homes that harmonize with nature.

Chapter 4: Indoor Air Quality and Organic Home Decor

Indoor plants not only add a touch of nature to your living spaces but also offer numerous health and environmental benefits, particularly in terms of air purification. Here are the key advantages of having indoor plants for improving air quality:

**1. Air Purification:

- **Mechanism:** Through a process known as phytoremediation, indoor plants absorb and metabolize pollutants from the air.
- **Benefits:**
    - Removes common indoor pollutants such as volatile organic compounds (VOCs), benzene, formaldehyde, and trichloroethylene.
    - Enhances overall indoor air quality, creating a healthier living environment.

**2. Oxygen Production:

- **Mechanism:** During photosynthesis, plants absorb carbon dioxide and release oxygen.
- **Benefits:**
    - Increases oxygen levels in indoor spaces, promoting better respiratory health.
    - Creates a more refreshing and oxygen-rich atmosphere.

**3. Humidity Regulation:

- **Mechanism:** Plants release water vapor during transpiration, helping to regulate humidity.
- **Benefits:**
    - Maintains optimal indoor humidity levels, preventing the air from becoming too dry.
    - Reduces the risk of respiratory issues and dry skin.

**4. Stress Reduction:

- **Mechanism:** The presence of indoor plants has been linked to stress reduction and improved mental well-being.
- **Benefits:**
    - Enhances mood and reduces stress levels.
    - Creates a calming and visually appealing indoor environment.

**5. Boosted Productivity and Focus:

- **Mechanism:** Studies have suggested that having plants in indoor spaces can enhance concentration and productivity.
- **Benefits:**
    - Improves cognitive function and attention.

o   Creates a more pleasant and conducive atmosphere for work or study.

**6. Reduced Sick Building Syndrome:

- **Mechanism:** Indoor plants can help mitigate the effects of sick building syndrome, a condition associated with poor indoor air quality.
- **Benefits:**
    o   Alleviates symptoms like headaches, fatigue, and respiratory issues.
    o   Supports a healthier indoor environment.

**7. Allergen Filtration:

- **Mechanism:** Plants can help filter out airborne allergens.
- **Benefits:**
    o   Reduces the presence of common allergens like dust and mold spores.
    o   Provides relief for individuals with allergies.

**8. Improved Sleep Quality:

- **Mechanism:** Some plants release oxygen even at night, contributing to improved sleep quality.
- **Benefits:**
    o   Creates a more restful sleep environment.
    o   Enhances overall sleep patterns and well-being.

**9. Aesthetically Pleasing Environment:

- **Mechanism:** The visual appeal of indoor plants contributes to a more aesthetically pleasing indoor environment.
- **Benefits:**
    o   Enhances the overall ambiance of living spaces.
    o   Adds a touch of nature to indoor decor.

**10. Easy Maintenance:

- **Mechanism:** Many indoor plants require minimal maintenance and can thrive in indoor conditions.
- **Benefits:**
    o   Suitable for individuals with varying levels of gardening expertise.
    o   Low-maintenance plants contribute to a hassle-free indoor gardening experience.

Conclusion:

Integrating indoor plants into your living spaces is a simple yet effective way to enhance air quality, promote well-being, and create a more visually appealing environment. With a diverse range of plants to choose from, it's possible to find options that suit various preferences and fit seamlessly into different indoor settings. Whether you have a spacious living room or a compact office, incorporating indoor plants is a natural and beneficial way to improve the quality of the air you breathe and the overall atmosphere of your indoor spaces.

The choice of indoor plants depends on various factors, including the specific conditions of each space in your home. Here are suggestions for suitable plants for different areas of the home:

**1. Living Room:

- **Suggestions:**
    - **Fiddle Leaf Fig (Ficus lyrata):** Adds a touch of elegance with large, glossy leaves.
    - **Snake Plant (Sansevieria):** Requires minimal care, known for air-purifying qualities.
    - **Spider Plant (Chlorophytum comosum):** Thrives in indirect light, helps remove pollutants.
    - **Peace Lily (Spathiphyllum):** Elegant and effective at purifying the air.

**2. Bedroom:

- **Suggestions:**
    - **Lavender (Lavandula):** Fragrant and promotes relaxation and better sleep.
    - **Aloe Vera:** Easy to care for and adds a touch of greenery.
    - **Jasmine (Jasminum):** Fragrant and known for its calming properties.
    - **Spider Plant (Chlorophytum comosum):** Cleans the air and thrives in low light.

**3. Kitchen:

- **Suggestions:**
    - **Herbs (Basil, Mint, Rosemary):** Functional and aromatic for cooking.
    - **Succulents:** Compact and easy to care for.
    - **African Violet (Saintpaulia):** Adds color and thrives in bright, indirect light.
    - **Snake Plant (Sansevieria):** Tolerant of varying light conditions.

**4. Bathroom:

- **Suggestions:**
    - **Ferns (Boston Fern, Maidenhair Fern):** Thrive in the high humidity of bathrooms.
    - **Snake Plant (Sansevieria):** Can tolerate low light conditions.
    - **Orchids:** Elegant and enjoy the humidity of bathrooms.
    - **Bamboo (Lucky Bamboo):** Adds a touch of greenery and thrives in low light.

**5. Home Office:

- **Suggestions:**

- o **ZZ Plant (Zamioculcas zamiifolia):** Low-maintenance and can tolerate low light.
  - o **Philodendron:** Comes in various varieties, adaptable to different light conditions.
  - o **Pothos (Epipremnum aureum):** Easy to care for and suitable for various light levels.
  - o **Rubber Plant (Ficus elastica):** Adds a statement and tolerates moderate light.

6. Hallway or Entryway:

- **Suggestions:**
  - o **Dracaena:** Comes in various varieties and adds height to the space.
  - o **Spider Plant (Chlorophytum comosum):** Suitable for hanging planters.
  - o **Succulents:** Compact and suitable for small spaces.
  - o **Money Plant (Epipremnum aureum):** Easy to care for and considered lucky.

7. Dark Corners:

- **Suggestions:**
  - o **ZZ Plant (Zamioculcas zamiifolia):** Thrives in low light conditions.
  - o **Snake Plant (Sansevieria):** Tolerant of low light and infrequent watering.
  - o **Peace Lily (Spathiphyllum):** Adapts well to low light and purifies the air.
  - o **Cast Iron Plant (Aspidistra elatior):** Hardy and suitable for low light.

8. Windowsills:

- **Suggestions:**
  - o **Herbs (Thyme, Parsley, Chives):** Convenient for culinary use.
  - o **African Violet (Saintpaulia):** Prefers indirect light on windowsills.
  - o **Succulents:** Enjoy the sunlight and are space-efficient.
  - o **Jade Plant (Crassula ovata):** Thrives in bright, indirect light.

9. Balcony or Patio:

- **Suggestions:**
  - o **Lavender (Lavandula):** Fragrant and attracts pollinators.
  - o **Geraniums:** Colorful and suitable for outdoor containers.
  - o **Citrus Trees (Lemon, Orange):** For sunny outdoor spaces.
  - o **Ferns:** Bring a lush, green look to outdoor areas with partial shade.

10. Shelves or Ledges:

- **Suggestions:**
  - o **String of Pearls (Senecio rowleyanus):** Trailing plant suitable for hanging or shelves.
  - o **Air Plants (Tillandsia):** Require no soil and can be placed on shelves.
  - o **Cactus:** Compact and easy to care for.

o   **Fittonia (Nerve Plant):** Adds vibrant colors and is suitable for small spaces.

Remember:

- Consider light conditions, humidity levels, and space constraints when choosing plants.
- Regularly water and provide appropriate care based on the specific needs of each plant.
- Grouping plants with similar care requirements can simplify maintenance.

Conclusion:

Choosing the right plants for different spaces in your home can enhance the overall atmosphere, aesthetics, and well-being of each room. By selecting plants that thrive in specific conditions, you can enjoy the benefits of indoor gardening while creating a more harmonious and inviting living environment.

Using organic materials in home decor is a sustainable and eco-friendly way to create a warm, natural, and healthy living environment. Organic materials are derived from natural sources and often have minimal environmental impact during production. Here are various organic materials commonly used in home decor:

**1. Wood:

- **Description:** Sustainably sourced and certified wood, such as bamboo, reclaimed wood, or FSC-certified timber.
- **Applications:**
    o   **Furniture:** Tables, chairs, bed frames.
    o   **Flooring:** Hardwood, bamboo, or cork flooring.
    o   **Decor Items:** Wooden bowls, trays, and wall art.

**2. Bamboo:

- **Description:** A fast-growing and renewable material.
- **Applications:**
    o   **Furniture:** Chairs, tables, shelving.
    o   **Textiles:** Bamboo fiber for bedding and curtains.
    o   **Decor Items:** Bamboo baskets, wall panels.

**3. Cork:

- **Description:** Harvested from the bark of cork oak trees without harming the tree.
- **Applications:**
    o   **Flooring:** Cork flooring.
    o   **Furniture:** Tables, chairs, and accessories.
    o   **Wall Coverings:** Cork tiles or panels.

**4. Natural Fibers:

- **Description:** Plant-based fibers like cotton, linen, jute, or hemp.
- **Applications:**
  - **Textiles:** Bedding, curtains, rugs.
  - **Furniture:** Upholstery made from natural fabrics.
  - **Decor Items:** Throw pillows, table runners.

**5. Stone:

- **Description:** Natural stone such as marble, granite, or slate.
- **Applications:**
  - **Countertops:** Marble or granite kitchen countertops.
  - **Flooring:** Natural stone tiles.
  - **Decor Items:** Stone sculptures, vases.

**6. Wool:

- **Description:** Natural fiber obtained from sheep.
- **Applications:**
  - **Textiles:** Wool rugs, blankets, and upholstery.
  - **Decor Items:** Wool throw pillows, wall hangings.

**7. Clay and Terracotta:

- **Description:** Earthen materials often used in pottery.
- **Applications:**
  - **Pottery:** Terracotta planters, vases.
  - **Tiles:** Terracotta tiles for flooring or backsplashes.
  - **Decor Items:** Clay sculptures, figurines.

**8. Seagrass:

- **Description:** A natural fiber obtained from seagrass plants.
- **Applications:**
  - **Furniture:** Seagrass chairs, ottomans.
  - **Rugs:** Seagrass rugs.
  - **Decor Items:** Baskets, lampshades.

**9. Recycled Glass:

- **Description:** Glass made from recycled materials.
- **Applications:**
  - **Decor Items:** Recycled glass vases, bowls.
  - **Lighting:** Recycled glass pendant lights.
  - **Tableware:** Glassware made from recycled glass.

**10. Hemp:

- **Description:** Fiber obtained from the hemp plant.
- **Applications:**
  - **Textiles:** Hemp fabric for curtains, bedding.
  - **Rugs:** Hemp rugs.
  - **Decor Items:** Hemp wall hangings, baskets.

11. Organic Cotton:

- **Description:** Cotton grown without synthetic pesticides or fertilizers.
- **Applications:**
  - **Textiles:** Organic cotton bedding, towels.
  - **Decor Items:** Organic cotton throw pillows, upholstery.

12. Sisal:

- **Description:** Natural fiber from the agave plant.
- **Applications:**
  - **Rugs:** Sisal rugs.
  - **Furniture:** Sisal-wrapped furniture.
  - **Decor Items:** Sisal baskets, wall art.

13. Cotton Canvas:

- **Description:** Sturdy, natural fabric made from cotton.
- **Applications:**
  - **Textiles:** Canvas wall art, upholstery.
  - **Decor Items:** Canvas prints, floor cushions.

14. Jute:

- **Description:** Natural fiber from the jute plant.
- **Applications:**
  - **Rugs:** Jute rugs.
  - **Decor Items:** Jute baskets, placemats.
  - **Furniture:** Jute-wrapped furniture.

15. Leather:

- **Description:** Natural material from animal hides.
- **Applications:**
  - **Furniture:** Leather chairs, sofas.
  - **Decor Items:** Leather cushions, poufs.
  - **Accessories:** Leather wall art, trays.

16. Wicker and Rattan:

- **Description:** Natural materials from weaving plant fibers.
- **Applications:**
  - **Furniture:** Wicker or rattan chairs, tables.
  - **Decor Items:** Wicker baskets, trays.
  - **Lighting:** Wicker pendant lights.

**17. Linen:

- **Description:** Fabric made from the flax plant.
- **Applications:**
  - **Textiles:** Linen curtains, bedding.
  - **Decor Items:** Linen throw pillows, table runners.
  - **Furniture:** Linen-upholstered chairs.

**18. Recycled or Reclaimed Wood:

- **Description:** Wood salvaged from old structures or repurposed materials.
- **Applications:**
  - **Furniture:** Reclaimed wood tables, shelves.
  - **Decor Items:** Wooden wall art, frames.
  - **Flooring:** Reclaimed wood flooring.

**19. Copper:

- **Description:** Metal with natural antibacterial properties.
- **Applications:**
  - **Decor Items:** Copper vases, candle holders.
  - **Kitchenware:** Copper pots, pans.
  - **Lighting:** Copper pendant lights.

**20. Silk:

- **Description:** Natural fiber produced by silkworms.
- **Applications:**
  - **Textiles:** Silk curtains, bedding.
  - **Decor Items:** Silk cushions, wall hangings.
  - **Accessories:** Silk table runners.

Benefits of Using Organic Materials in Home Decor:

- **Sustainability:** Organic materials are often renewable, biodegradable, and have a lower environmental impact.
- **Health:** Many organic materials contribute to a healthier indoor environment by avoiding harmful chemicals.
- **Aesthetics:** Organic materials often bring a natural and timeless aesthetic to home decor.

- **Connection with Nature:** Using materials like wood, bamboo, or plants fosters a connection with nature.

Conclusion:

Integrating organic materials into home decor not only enhances the visual appeal of your living spaces but also aligns with sustainable and environmentally conscious living. Whether it's furniture, textiles, or decor items, there are numerous options to choose from that cater to both style and eco-friendliness.

Organic fabrics offer a range of benefits, both in terms of environmental sustainability and personal health. Additionally, they often bring a natural and aesthetically pleasing touch to various items, from clothing to home textiles. Here are the key benefits and aesthetics of organic fabrics:

Benefits of Organic Fabrics:

**1. Environmental Sustainability:

- **No Chemical Pesticides:** Organic fabrics are produced without the use of synthetic pesticides, reducing harm to the environment and ecosystems.
- **No Synthetic Fertilizers:** Organic farming avoids the use of synthetic fertilizers, preventing soil and water contamination.

**2. Reduced Water Usage:

- **Water Conservation:** Organic farming practices often prioritize water conservation and efficient use compared to conventional methods.

**3. Healthier Soil:

- **Soil Health:** Organic farming promotes soil fertility through practices like crop rotation and the use of organic matter, enhancing long-term soil health.

**4. Biodegradability:

- **Less Environmental Impact:** Organic fabrics are typically biodegradable, reducing their impact on landfills at the end of their lifecycle.

**5. Reduced Impact on Wildlife:

- **Biodiversity:** Organic farming practices aim to preserve biodiversity, minimizing disruption to ecosystems and wildlife.

**6. Health Benefits:

- **Reduced Chemical Exposure:** Organic fabrics are free from harmful chemicals often found in conventionally produced textiles, reducing the risk of skin irritation and allergic reactions.

**7. Social Responsibility:

- **Fair Labor Practices:** Many organic fabric producers adhere to fair labor practices, ensuring ethical treatment and fair wages for workers.

Aesthetics of Organic Fabrics:

**1. Softness and Comfort:

- **Natural Feel:** Organic fabrics, especially those like organic cotton and linen, often have a soft and comfortable feel against the skin.

**2. Breathability:

- **Air Circulation:** Organic fabrics, such as cotton and linen, are known for their breathability, making them suitable for warm weather and active wear.

**3. Texture and Variety:

- **Natural Texture:** Organic fabrics often retain a natural texture, enhancing the overall aesthetic of clothing and home textiles.
- **Variety:** Organic fabrics come in various textures and weaves, providing options for different styles and preferences.

**4. Earth-Toned Colors:

- **Natural Colors:** Organic fabrics may feature earthy, natural tones, contributing to a more organic and eco-friendly aesthetic.

**5. Durability:

- **Quality Construction:** Well-made organic fabrics can be durable and long-lasting, offering a timeless appeal.

**6. Unique Patterns:

- **Artisanal Touch:** Some organic fabrics, especially those produced through traditional methods, may feature unique patterns and designs, adding an artisanal touch to the final product.

**7. Timeless Style:

- **Versatility:** Organic fabrics are often versatile and timeless, fitting into various style preferences and enduring changing fashion trends.

**8. Natural Luster:

- **Sheen:** Fabrics like silk, when produced organically, may retain a natural luster, adding elegance to clothing and home decor.

**9. Soft Drape:

- **Graceful Drape:** Fabrics like organic cotton and Tencel can have a soft and graceful drape, enhancing the flow of clothing and drapery.

**10. Unique Characteristics:

- **Nubby Textures:** Fabrics like organic linen may exhibit nubby textures, providing a distinct and rustic appearance.

Conclusion:

Organic fabrics offer a harmonious blend of environmental responsibility and aesthetic appeal. Choosing organic textiles not only supports sustainable and ethical practices but also allows individuals to enjoy the comfort, breathability, and unique aesthetic qualities that organic fabrics often bring to clothing, bedding, and other textile products. The increasing availability of organic options in the market allows consumers to make conscious choices that align with their values and contribute to a more sustainable and mindful lifestyle.

Numerous studies have investigated the link between indoor air quality (IAQ) and human health. Poor indoor air quality can have various adverse effects on respiratory, cardiovascular, and overall well-being. Here's an overview of key findings from relevant studies:

**1. Respiratory Health:

**a. Asthma:

- **Study:** "Indoor Environmental Factors and Health: Asthma and Allergy" (NIEHS)
- **Findings:** Exposure to indoor pollutants such as mold, dust mites, and pet dander can exacerbate asthma symptoms and contribute to the development of asthma in susceptible individuals.

**b. Indoor Allergens:

- **Study:** "Indoor Allergens: Relevance to Airborne Allergic Disease" (Journal of Allergy and Clinical Immunology)
- **Findings:** Indoor allergens, including those from dust mites, pets, and cockroaches, can lead to allergic reactions and worsen respiratory conditions.

****c. Secondhand Smoke:**

- **Study:** "Health Effects of Passive Smoking: 10 Years of Progress" (U.S. Surgeon General's Report)
- **Findings:** Exposure to secondhand smoke indoors is associated with respiratory infections, asthma exacerbation, and sudden infant death syndrome (SIDS).

**2. Cardiovascular Health:

****a. Particulate Matter (PM):**

- **Study:** "Ambient Air Pollution and Cardiovascular Disease: A Comprehensive Review and Meta-Analysis" (European Heart Journal)
- **Findings:** Exposure to fine particulate matter (PM2.5) is linked to an increased risk of cardiovascular diseases, including heart attacks and strokes.

****b. Volatile Organic Compounds (VOCs):**

- **Study:** "Indoor Air Pollution: The Role of Indoor Chemical Exposures in the Development of Chronic Obstructive Pulmonary Disease" (Current Opinion in Allergy and Clinical Immunology)
- **Findings:** Indoor exposure to VOCs, often emitted by household products, is associated with an increased risk of respiratory diseases and may contribute to cardiovascular issues.

**3. Cognitive Function and Productivity:

****a. Indoor CO2 Levels:**

- **Study:** "Associations of Cognitive Function Scores with Carbon Dioxide, Ventilation, and Volatile Organic Compound Exposures in Office Workers: A Controlled Exposure Study of Green and Conventional Office Environments" (Environmental Health Perspectives)
- **Findings:** Higher levels of indoor carbon dioxide (CO2) are associated with reduced cognitive function and decision-making performance in office environments.

****b. Sick Building Syndrome:**

- **Study:** "Indoor Environmental Quality in Green vs. Conventional Office Buildings: Associations with Cognitive Function" (Building and Environment)
- **Findings:** Indoor environmental quality, including factors like ventilation and lighting, can impact cognitive function and productivity, contributing to "sick building syndrome."

**4. Pregnancy and Childhood Health:

****a. Maternal Exposure:**

- **Study:** "Indoor Air Pollution and Adverse Pregnancy Outcomes: A Review" (Reproductive Sciences)
- **Findings:** Maternal exposure to indoor air pollutants during pregnancy is associated with adverse outcomes, including preterm birth and low birth weight.

b. Childhood Respiratory Health:

- **Study:** "Indoor Air Quality in Homes and the Risk of Allergic Rhinitis in Children" (Pediatric Allergy and Immunology)
- **Findings:** Poor indoor air quality is linked to an increased risk of allergic rhinitis and respiratory symptoms in children.

Conclusion:

The evidence from these studies underscores the critical importance of maintaining good indoor air quality for overall health. Common indoor pollutants, such as particulate matter, allergens, and volatile organic compounds, can have wide-ranging effects on respiratory, cardiovascular, and cognitive health. Implementing measures to improve indoor air quality, such as adequate ventilation, regular cleaning, and reducing exposure to indoor pollutants, is crucial for creating a healthier indoor environment.

Organic practices can significantly contribute to better air quality by promoting sustainable agricultural and lifestyle choices that minimize the release of harmful pollutants. Here are several ways in which organic practices positively impact air quality:

1. Reduced Use of Synthetic Pesticides and Fertilizers:

- **Organic Agriculture:** Avoids the use of synthetic pesticides and fertilizers, which can release harmful chemicals into the air when sprayed or applied to crops.
- **Impact:** Reducing the use of these chemicals minimizes air pollution and prevents the dispersal of airborne toxins.

2. Prevention of Soil Erosion:

- **Organic Farming Techniques:** Focus on soil conservation measures, such as cover cropping and crop rotation, to prevent soil erosion.
- **Impact:** Minimizing soil erosion helps maintain air quality by preventing the release of dust particles and pollutants into the atmosphere.

3. Carbon Sequestration:

- **Organic Practices:** Emphasize the use of cover crops and organic matter, enhancing soil health and promoting carbon sequestration.
- **Impact:** Increased carbon sequestration helps mitigate climate change, reducing the concentration of greenhouse gases in the atmosphere.

4. Promotion of Agroforestry:

- **Organic Farming Systems:** Often incorporate agroforestry practices, planting trees alongside crops.
- **Impact:** Trees absorb pollutants, release oxygen, and contribute to a healthier atmosphere, thereby improving air quality.

5. Use of Organic Inputs:

- **Organic Inputs:** Include natural fertilizers, compost, and organic amendments that release fewer pollutants compared to synthetic counterparts.
- **Impact:** Reducing the reliance on chemical inputs minimizes the release of harmful substances into the air.

6. No Genetically Modified Organisms (GMOs):

- **Organic Standards:** Prohibit the use of genetically modified organisms (GMOs).
- **Impact:** Preventing the cultivation of GMOs can contribute to air quality by avoiding potential environmental risks associated with genetic modification.

7. Sustainable Livestock Practices:

- **Organic Livestock Farming:** Emphasizes humane treatment and sustainable practices, reducing the environmental impact of conventional concentrated animal feeding operations (CAFOs).
- **Impact:** Minimizing air pollution associated with industrial-scale livestock farming contributes to better overall air quality.

8. Avoidance of Synthetic Hormones and Antibiotics:

- **Organic Livestock Production:** Prohibits the use of synthetic hormones and antibiotics.
- **Impact:** Preventing the release of antibiotic residues into the environment helps maintain the quality of air and water.

9. Encouragement of Local and Sustainable Practices:

- **Organic Principles:** Often align with local and sustainable agriculture, reducing the carbon footprint associated with long-distance transportation.
- **Impact:** Supporting local and sustainable practices helps decrease air pollution caused by transportation-related emissions.

10. Reduced Fossil Fuel Dependency:

- **Organic Agriculture:** Often employs practices that reduce reliance on fossil fuels, such as minimal tillage and the use of cover crops.

- **Impact:** Lowering fossil fuel usage in agriculture helps decrease air pollution associated with the extraction, processing, and burning of fossil fuels.

11. Support for Biodiversity:

- **Organic Farming:** Promotes biodiversity, creating healthier ecosystems.
- **Impact:** Healthy ecosystems contribute to improved air quality by maintaining ecological balance and reducing the risk of air pollution.

Conclusion:

By adopting organic practices, individuals and agricultural communities contribute to better air quality by minimizing the use of harmful chemicals, promoting sustainable farming techniques, and supporting a holistic approach to environmental stewardship. These practices not only benefit the health of ecosystems but also contribute to the overall well-being of communities and the planet.

Organic practices can significantly contribute to better air quality by promoting sustainable agricultural methods and reducing the use of synthetic chemicals. Here are several ways in which organic practices positively impact air quality:

1. Reduced Use of Synthetic Pesticides and Fertilizers:

- **Organic Agriculture:** Avoids synthetic pesticides and fertilizers.
- **Impact:** Reduces the release of airborne pollutants associated with the production and application of chemical inputs.

2. No Genetically Modified Organisms (GMOs):

- **Organic Standards:** Prohibit the use of genetically modified organisms.
- **Impact:** Helps prevent potential environmental risks and uncertainties associated with genetically modified crops.

3. Soil Health and Carbon Sequestration:

- **Organic Farming Techniques:** Focus on improving soil health through practices like cover cropping and crop rotation.
- **Impact:** Healthy soils sequester carbon, contributing to climate change mitigation and reducing the release of greenhouse gases into the atmosphere.

4. Agroforestry Practices:

- **Organic Farming Systems:** Often incorporate agroforestry, planting trees alongside crops.
- **Impact:** Trees absorb pollutants, release oxygen, and contribute to improved air quality.

5. Sustainable Livestock Management:

- **Organic Livestock Farming:** Emphasizes humane treatment and sustainable practices.
- **Impact:** Reduces air pollution associated with concentrated animal feeding operations (CAFOs) in conventional livestock farming.

6. No Antibiotics or Synthetic Hormones:

- **Organic Livestock Production:** Prohibits the use of synthetic hormones and antibiotics.
- **Impact:** Prevents the release of antibiotic residues into the environment, contributing to better air quality.

7. Encouragement of Local and Sustainable Practices:

- **Organic Principles:** Often align with local and sustainable agriculture, reducing the carbon footprint associated with long-distance transportation.
- **Impact:** Promotes environmentally friendly transportation practices, decreasing air pollution from the transport of goods.

8. Reduced Fossil Fuel Dependency:

- **Organic Agriculture:** Often employs practices that reduce reliance on fossil fuels, such as minimal tillage and the use of cover crops.
- **Impact:** Lowering fossil fuel usage in agriculture helps decrease air pollution associated with the extraction, processing, and burning of fossil fuels.

9. Biodiversity Conservation:

- **Organic Farming:** Promotes biodiversity, avoiding monoculture and supporting diverse ecosystems.
- **Impact:** Healthy ecosystems contribute to improved air quality by maintaining ecological balance.

10. Promotion of Sustainable Practices:

- **Organic Certification:** Encourages farmers to adopt sustainable practices beyond the avoidance of synthetic chemicals.
- **Impact:** Sustainable practices, such as efficient resource use and waste reduction, contribute to overall environmental health and air quality.

11. Reduction of Airborne Agricultural Emissions:

- **Avoidance of Synthetic Nitrogen:** Organic farming typically avoids the use of synthetic nitrogen fertilizers.

- **Impact:** Reduces emissions of nitrogen oxides, which contribute to air pollution and can have adverse effects on respiratory health.

Conclusion:

Organic practices play a crucial role in promoting environmental sustainability and contributing to better air quality. By avoiding synthetic chemicals, prioritizing soil health, and supporting diverse ecosystems, organic agriculture fosters a healthier environment for both ecosystems and communities. As consumers and farmers increasingly embrace organic practices, the positive impact on air quality becomes an important component of sustainable and regenerative agriculture.

While specific stories of homes with improved air quality through organic home decor may be limited, there are numerous anecdotes and examples that highlight the positive effects of incorporating organic elements into home design. Here are a few illustrative scenarios:

1. The Green Apartment:

- **Story:** Jane, a resident in a city apartment, decided to transform her living space into a "green oasis." She introduced indoor plants, organic cotton curtains, and natural fiber rugs. Over time, she noticed a significant improvement in the air quality within her apartment. The indoor plants not only added a touch of nature but also acted as natural air purifiers, reducing pollutants and enhancing the overall well-being of the space.

2. Natural Materials Makeover:

- **Story:** The Smith family opted for a home makeover using organic and natural materials. They replaced synthetic carpets with wool rugs, chose organic cotton beddings, and incorporated wooden furniture finished with non-toxic, organic sealants. The result was a home with improved indoor air quality. The absence of off-gassing from synthetic materials created a fresher and healthier living environment for the entire family.

3. The Eco-Friendly Renovation:

- **Story:** Mark and Sarah decided to renovate their home using sustainable and organic materials. They chose low-VOC (volatile organic compound) paints, reclaimed wood for flooring, and organic linens for upholstery. The improved indoor air quality was noticeable, especially after the renovation, as the use of eco-friendly materials contributed to a reduction in harmful off-gassing, creating a healthier living space.

4. Natural Textiles in the Suburbs:

- **Story:** The Johnsons, living in a suburban home, decided to switch to organic textiles for their window treatments and upholstery. By choosing organic cotton and linen, they not only embraced a more sustainable lifestyle but also experienced an improvement in air quality. The decision to avoid synthetic fabrics reduced the presence of VOCs in their home, leading to a fresher and more breathable atmosphere.

5. The Wellness Retreat:

- **Story:** Alex, a wellness enthusiast, designed his home as a personal retreat using organic and natural elements. From organic mattresses to indoor plants and natural beeswax candles, every element was chosen with air quality in mind. Visitors often commented on the fresh and inviting atmosphere, contributing to a sense of well-being and relaxation.

6. The Sustainable Tiny House:

- **Story:** Emily embraced a minimalist and sustainable lifestyle by moving into a tiny house. She opted for natural and organic materials in her compact living space, such as organic bedding, reclaimed wood furniture, and indoor plants. The small size of the house made it easier to maintain good air quality, and the intentional use of organic elements added to the overall sense of purity and cleanliness.

Conclusion:

While these stories are fictional, they are inspired by real-world examples of individuals and families making conscious choices to improve indoor air quality through organic home decor. The growing awareness of the impact of our living environments on health has led many people to explore organic and sustainable options, contributing to homes that not only look beautiful but also support a healthier and more sustainable lifestyle.

Adopting an organic in-home environment offers a holistic approach to sustainable living, providing numerous benefits for both individuals and the planet. The key findings and holistic benefits can be summarized as follows:

1. Improved Air Quality:

- **Key Finding:** Organic practices in the home, including the use of natural materials and the incorporation of indoor plants, contribute to reduced indoor air pollution.
- **Holistic Benefit:** Enhanced air quality supports respiratory health, reduces the risk of allergies, and creates a fresher and more inviting living space.

2. Sustainable Agriculture Practices:

- **Key Finding:** Organic farming practices, whether in the kitchen or backyard, prioritize sustainability, avoiding synthetic pesticides and fertilizers.
- **Holistic Benefit:** By supporting organic agriculture, individuals contribute to healthier ecosystems, reduce environmental impact, and promote sustainable food systems.

3. Health and Well-Being:

- **Key Finding:** Choosing organic materials for home decor, clothing, and bedding reduces exposure to harmful chemicals, promoting overall well-being.
- **Holistic Benefit:** Organic living fosters a healthier lifestyle by minimizing the risk of skin irritation, allergic reactions, and potential long-term health issues associated with synthetic chemicals.

4. Climate Change Mitigation:

- **Key Finding:** Organic practices, including carbon sequestration in organic soils, contribute to mitigating climate change.
- **Holistic Benefit:** By adopting organic principles, individuals play a role in reducing greenhouse gas emissions and supporting a more sustainable and resilient planet.

5. Biodiversity and Ecosystem Health:

- **Key Finding:** Organic farming encourages biodiversity, preserving natural habitats and ecosystems.
- **Holistic Benefit:** Promoting biodiversity supports ecological balance, protects pollinators, and contributes to the health of the entire ecosystem.

6. Local and Sustainable Living:

- **Key Finding:** Choosing locally sourced and sustainable products reduces the carbon footprint associated with transportation.
- **Holistic Benefit:** Embracing local and sustainable living practices supports local economies, reduces environmental impact, and contributes to a more resilient and connected community.

7. Reduced Fossil Fuel Dependency:

- **Key Finding:** Organic farming often employs practices that reduce reliance on fossil fuels.
- **Holistic Benefit:** Lowering fossil fuel usage in agriculture contributes to decreased air pollution, supports a cleaner environment, and addresses climate change.

8. Connection with Nature:

- **Key Finding:** Integrating natural elements into home decor, such as indoor plants and organic materials, fosters a deeper connection with nature.
- **Holistic Benefit:** Increased exposure to nature positively impacts mental health, reduces stress, and enhances overall quality of life.

Conclusion:

In conclusion, embracing an organic in-home environment goes beyond individual lifestyle choices; it represents a commitment to a sustainable and mindful way of living. The holistic benefits extend to personal health, environmental conservation, and a more harmonious relationship with the natural world. By making conscious choices in daily practices, individuals contribute to a more resilient and sustainable future for themselves and generations to come.

The importance of ongoing vigilance and adaptation to changing circumstances cannot be overstated in the context of maintaining an organic in-home environment. While adopting organic practices is a commendable and positive step towards sustainable living, staying vigilant and adaptable is crucial for several reasons:

1. Emerging Environmental Challenges:

- **Reason:** Environmental challenges, such as climate change and evolving pollution sources, require continuous attention.
- **Importance:** Staying vigilant enables individuals to adapt their practices in response to new challenges and contribute effectively to ongoing environmental conservation efforts.

2. Advancements in Sustainable Practices:

- **Reason:** Research and innovations in sustainable living are ongoing, leading to the discovery of new and improved practices.
- **Importance:** Remaining vigilant allows individuals to stay informed about advancements and adapt their lifestyle choices to align with the most effective and sustainable practices.

3. Dynamic Health Considerations:

- **Reason:** Health-related knowledge evolves, and new considerations may emerge over time.
- **Importance:** Ongoing vigilance ensures that individuals can adapt their habits to the latest health recommendations, enhancing personal well-being in the ever-changing landscape of health information.

4. Local and Global Economic Shifts:

- **Reason:** Economic landscapes, both locally and globally, are subject to changes that may impact the availability and affordability of organic products.
- **Importance:** Being vigilant allows individuals to adapt their choices based on economic shifts, supporting local and sustainable options even in changing financial climates.

5. Technological Innovations:

- **Reason:** Technology continually evolves, offering new solutions for sustainable living and home practices.
- **Importance:** Staying vigilant enables individuals to incorporate eco-friendly technologies into their homes, enhancing efficiency and reducing environmental impact.

6. Community and Social Dynamics:

- **Reason:** Social and community norms may change, influencing the collective approach to sustainable living.
- **Importance:** Being adaptable allows individuals to engage with and contribute to evolving social expectations, fostering a sense of community and shared responsibility.

7. Personal Lifestyle Changes:

- **Reason:** Individuals undergo life changes, such as moving, starting a family, or transitioning to a different career.
- **Importance:** Ongoing vigilance helps individuals adapt their sustainable practices to align with new lifestyle circumstances, ensuring that eco-conscious choices remain feasible and relevant.

8. Global Events and Crises:

- **Reason:** Global events, such as pandemics or natural disasters, can impact supply chains and access to organic products.
- **Importance:** Remaining vigilant allows individuals to adapt their sustainable practices during crises, making informed decisions that support both personal and global resilience.

Conclusion:

In the dynamic and interconnected world we live in, embracing an organic in-home environment is an ongoing journey that requires vigilance and adaptability. By staying informed, remaining open to change, and adjusting practices in response to evolving circumstances, individuals can ensure that their commitment to sustainability remains effective, relevant, and impactful. This ongoing vigilance not only benefits personal well-being but also contributes to a collective effort in building a more sustainable and resilient future

A comprehensive investigation into creating a safe in-home environment.

Introduction

Creating a safe in-home environment is a fundamental aspect of fostering well-being, comfort, and security for individuals and families. The home should be a sanctuary where one feels protected, both physically and emotionally. The importance of a safe in-home environment extends across various dimensions, encompassing health, mental well-being, and overall quality of life. Here's an introduction to why a safe home is paramount:

**1. Physical Safety:

- A safe home provides a protective space, minimizing the risk of accidents, injuries, and potential hazards.
- Elements such as secure staircases, childproofing measures, and well-maintained infrastructure contribute to physical safety.

**2. Mental Health and Well-Being:

- A secure home environment plays a crucial role in promoting mental health by offering a sense of stability and refuge.
- Minimizing stressors and creating a positive atmosphere at home can contribute to emotional well-being.

**3. Security and Privacy:

- Feeling safe in one's home is synonymous with security and privacy.
- Adequate security measures, such as robust locks, alarms, and well-lit exteriors, enhance the overall safety of the living space.

**4. Disease Prevention:

- A safe home includes measures to prevent the spread of diseases and maintain a healthy living environment.
- Proper sanitation, ventilation, and cleanliness contribute to the prevention of illnesses.

**5. Comfort and Quality of Life:

- Safety and comfort go hand in hand, creating an environment where individuals can relax and thrive.

- Features such as well-designed furniture, appropriate lighting, and temperature control enhance overall comfort.

**6. Accident Prevention:

- Ensuring a safe home involves proactive measures to prevent accidents, particularly for children and seniors.
- Safeguarding against slips, falls, and other potential accidents contributes to a secure living space.

**7. Adaptability to Changing Circumstances:

- A safe home is adaptable to changing circumstances, whether it be accommodating new family members, evolving health needs, or unexpected events.
- Flexibility in the home environment ensures continued safety and well-being.

**8. Resilience to Natural Disasters:

- Safety measures extend to preparedness for natural disasters, ensuring that homes are resilient to events like earthquakes, floods, or storms.
- Disaster-resistant construction and emergency preparedness contribute to the overall safety of the home.

Conclusion:

In essence, the importance of a safe in-home environment lies in its ability to serve as a haven, promoting physical health, mental well-being, and an enhanced quality of life. By prioritizing safety measures, individuals and families create a foundation for comfort, security, and resilience within the walls of their homes.

Creating a safe in-home environment involves identifying and mitigating potential hazards and risks that could compromise the well-being of individuals and families. These risks can vary depending on factors such as the home's location, structure, and the composition of its occupants. Here's an overview of potential hazards and risks that may exist in a home:

**1. Tripping Hazards:

- **Risk:** Loose rugs, cluttered walkways, or uneven flooring can lead to trips and falls.
- **Mitigation:** Secure rugs, keep walkways clear, and address any uneven surfaces.

**2. Electrical Issues:

- **Risk:** Damaged wiring, overloaded circuits, or faulty electrical appliances can pose fire hazards.
- **Mitigation:** Regularly inspect wiring, avoid overloading outlets, and promptly address electrical issues.

3. Fire Hazards:

- **Risk:** Unattended candles, faulty wiring, or cooking accidents can lead to fires.
- **Mitigation:** Install smoke detectors, have fire extinguishers, and follow fire safety practices.

4. Poor Indoor Air Quality:

- **Risk:** Indoor pollutants, inadequate ventilation, or mold can compromise air quality.
- **Mitigation:** Ensure proper ventilation, use air purifiers, and address moisture issues promptly.

5. Chemical Exposure:

- **Risk:** Exposure to harmful chemicals in cleaning products, paints, or pesticides.
- **Mitigation:** Choose eco-friendly and non-toxic products, ventilate when using chemicals, and store them safely.

6. Inadequate Security:

- **Risk:** Weak locks, poor lighting, or lack of security measures can make the home vulnerable to break-ins.
- **Mitigation:** Strengthen security measures, install quality locks, and consider home security systems.

7. Drowning Risks:

- **Risk:** Unsecured pools, bathtubs, or water features pose a risk, especially for children.
- **Mitigation:** Install proper barriers, never leave children unattended around water, and teach water safety.

8. Gas Leaks:

- **Risk:** Gas leaks from appliances or heating systems can lead to health hazards and explosions.
- **Mitigation:** Regularly check gas appliances, install carbon monoxide detectors, and address leaks promptly.

9. Structural Issues:

- **Risk:** Unstable foundations, deteriorating structures, or poorly maintained roofs can pose safety risks.
- **Mitigation:** Regularly inspect the home's structure, address maintenance issues promptly, and seek professional assessments.

10. Poisoning Risks:

- **Risk:** Ingesting harmful substances, such as medications or household chemicals.
- **Mitigation:** Store medications and chemicals out of reach, use childproof locks, and properly label substances.

11. Natural Disasters:

- **Risk:** Vulnerability to earthquakes, floods, hurricanes, or tornadoes depending on the geographical location.
- **Mitigation:** Prepare emergency kits, have evacuation plans, and reinforce the home against specific risks.

12. Radon Exposure:

- **Risk:** Radon, a colorless and odorless gas, can seep into homes from the ground, leading to health risks.
- **Mitigation:** Test for radon and, if necessary, install radon mitigation systems.

Conclusion:

Addressing potential hazards and risks in the home requires a proactive approach, regular assessments, and timely mitigation efforts. By identifying and mitigating these risks, individuals can create a safer and more secure living environment for themselves and their families.

Creating a safe home extends beyond the walls of the house; the outdoor space is equally important. Ensuring the safety of the outside of the house involves addressing potential hazards and implementing preventive measures. Here are key ways to make the outside of the house safe:

1. Well-Lit Exterior:

- **Implementation:** Install outdoor lighting along pathways, near entrances, and in the backyard.
- **Purpose:** Adequate lighting enhances visibility, deters intruders, and reduces the risk of trips and falls.

2. Secure Entrances:

- **Implementation:** Reinforce doors and windows with strong locks and deadbolts.
- **Purpose:** Enhancing security at entry points minimizes the risk of break-ins and unauthorized access.

3. Landscaping Safety:

- **Implementation:** Trim overgrown bushes, trees, and hedges regularly.

- **Purpose:** Well-maintained landscaping improves visibility, reduces hiding spots for intruders, and prevents pests.

4. Sturdy Outdoor Furniture:

- **Implementation:** Use durable and stable outdoor furniture.
- **Purpose:** Sturdy furniture minimizes the risk of accidents and injuries, especially during windy or inclement weather.

5. Anti-Slip Surfaces:

- **Implementation:** Choose slip-resistant materials for outdoor surfaces.
- **Purpose:** Prevent slips and falls by ensuring that decks, patios, and walkways have textures or coatings for traction.

6. Properly Maintained Walkways:

- **Implementation:** Repair any cracks or uneven surfaces on pathways.
- **Purpose:** Smooth and well-maintained walkways reduce tripping hazards.

7. Pool Safety Measures:

- **Implementation:** Install a fence around the pool with a self-latching gate.
- **Purpose:** Prevent accidental drownings by securing access to the pool area.

8. Secure Outdoor Storage:

- **Implementation:** Use lockable sheds or storage units for tools and equipment.
- **Purpose:** Minimize the risk of theft and ensure the safe storage of potentially dangerous tools.

9. Fire Safety Precautions:

- **Implementation:** Keep a safe distance between the house and outdoor fire features.
- **Purpose:** Prevent the risk of fires spreading to the house or other structures.

10. Clear Signage:

- **Implementation:** Install clear and visible address numbers.
- **Purpose:** Aid emergency services in locating the house quickly.

11. Pet Safety Measures:

- **Implementation:** Create secure enclosures for pets.

- **Purpose:** Prevent pets from wandering into unsafe areas or interacting with potentially harmful wildlife.

12. Weather-Resistant Materials:

- **Implementation:** Choose materials that can withstand local weather conditions.
- **Purpose:** Ensure the longevity and stability of outdoor structures, preventing weather-related hazards.

13. Regular Inspection and Maintenance:

- **Implementation:** Conduct routine inspections of outdoor areas.
- **Purpose:** Identify and address potential hazards promptly to maintain a safe environment.

14. Security Cameras:

- **Implementation:** Install outdoor security cameras.
- **Purpose:** Deter potential intruders and provide surveillance for added security.

15. Emergency Evacuation Plan:

- **Implementation:** Develop and communicate an emergency evacuation plan.
- **Purpose:** Ensure everyone in the household knows how to evacuate safely in case of emergencies.

By addressing these aspects, homeowners can create a safer outdoor environment, promoting both security and well-being for everyone in and around the house.

Ensuring safety around the property is essential to create a secure environment for residents and visitors. This involves addressing potential hazards and implementing preventive measures to minimize the risk of accidents, intrusions, or other safety concerns. Here are key considerations for maintaining safety around the property:

1. Perimeter Security:

- **Implementation:** Install fencing, walls, or natural barriers to define the property boundaries.
- **Purpose:** Clearly marked perimeters contribute to security and discourage unauthorized access.

2. Gated Access:

- **Implementation:** Use gates with secure locks and access control mechanisms.
- **Purpose:** Controlled access enhances security and prevents unauthorized entry.

3. Landscaping Safety:

- **Implementation:** Regularly trim vegetation, bushes, and trees around the property.
- **Purpose:** Well-maintained landscaping improves visibility, reduces hiding spots, and minimizes the risk of pests.

4. Lighting:

- **Implementation:** Install outdoor lighting along the property's perimeter.
- **Purpose:** Adequate lighting discourages intruders, enhances visibility, and promotes safety.

5. Security Cameras:

- **Implementation:** Install surveillance cameras at strategic points around the property.
- **Purpose:** Surveillance cameras act as a deterrent and provide documentation in case of security incidents.

6. Secure Gates and Garage Doors:

- **Implementation:** Ensure that gates and garage doors are in good working condition and have reliable locks.
- **Purpose:** Well-maintained entrances prevent unauthorized access and enhance overall property security.

7. Driveway Safety:

- **Implementation:** Keep driveways clear of obstacles and well-maintained.
- **Purpose:** A clear driveway minimizes tripping hazards and ensures easy access for emergency vehicles.

8. Clear Signage:

- **Implementation:** Use visible and clear signs to indicate private property, potential hazards, and emergency exits.
- **Purpose:** Clear signage enhances communication and contributes to overall safety awareness.

9. Pool Safety:

- **Implementation:** Install a secure fence around the pool area with a self-latching gate.
- **Purpose:** Prevent accidental drownings and ensure the safety of residents and visitors.

10. Emergency Contact Information:

- **Implementation:** Display emergency contact information in a visible location.
- **Purpose:** Ensure that residents, guests, and emergency services can quickly access essential contact details.

11. Secure Outdoor Storage:

- **Implementation:** Use lockable sheds or storage units for tools and equipment.
- **Purpose:** Secure storage prevents theft and ensures the safekeeping of potentially dangerous tools.

12. Mail and Package Security:

- **Implementation:** Secure mailboxes and consider using package delivery lockers.
- **Purpose:** Minimize the risk of mail theft and package pilfering.

13. Fire Safety Measures:

- **Implementation:** Create a defensible space by clearing combustible materials around the property.
- **Purpose:** Reduce the risk of wildfires spreading to the property.

14. Regular Inspections:

- **Implementation:** Conduct routine inspections of the property for potential hazards.
- **Purpose:** Proactive inspections help identify and address safety concerns promptly.

15. Neighborhood Watch:

- **Implementation:** Encourage community involvement in a neighborhood watch program.
- **Purpose:** Collaborative efforts enhance overall security and safety within the neighborhood.

16. Community Engagement:

- **Implementation:** Foster a sense of community through events, communication channels, and shared safety initiatives.
- **Purpose:** Engaged communities are more likely to work together for the safety of the entire neighborhood.

17. Emergency Evacuation Plan:

- **Implementation:** Develop and communicate an emergency evacuation plan for the property.
- **Purpose:** Ensure that residents and visitors know how to evacuate safely in case of emergencies.

By implementing these safety measures around the property, homeowners contribute to a secure and protected living environment. Regular vigilance, community engagement, and proactive measures enhance overall safety for everyone in the vicinity.

Checking and maintaining the fencing around your property is crucial for security, safety, and the overall well-being of your home. A well-maintained fence serves as a deterrent to intruders, defines property boundaries, and contributes to the overall aesthetics of your outdoor space. Here's a guide on checking and maintaining your property's fencing:

**1. Regular Inspections:

- **Frequency:** Conduct thorough inspections at least twice a year.
- **Purpose:** Identify any signs of wear, damage, or vulnerability in the fence.

**2. Check for Signs of Wear:

- **Indicators:** Look for rust, corrosion, or general wear on metal fences. Check for rot or warping in wooden fences.
- **Action:** Replace or repair any damaged or worn sections promptly.

**3. Inspect Fence Posts:

- **Focus:** Pay special attention to the stability of fence posts.
- **Action:** Ensure that posts are firmly anchored in the ground. Replace any loose or leaning posts.

**4. Examine Gate Functionality:

- **Functionality Check:** Open and close gates to ensure smooth operation.
- **Action:** Lubricate hinges if needed. Repair or replace any gates that are sagging or not closing properly.

**5. Secure Fence Rails:

- **Check:** Ensure that horizontal rails are securely attached.
- **Action:** Tighten loose rails and replace any that are damaged or weakened.

**6. Look for Pest Damage:

- **Indicators:** Check for signs of pest damage, such as termites or carpenter ants.
- **Action:** Treat any pest infestations promptly and repair or replace damaged sections.

**7. Inspect for Rot (Wooden Fences):

- **Focus:** Wooden fences are susceptible to rot, especially in humid or wet conditions.

- **Action:** Replace any rotted sections and consider applying a protective sealant to prevent future rot.

8. Verify Height and Visibility:

- **Requirement:** Ensure that the fence is of the appropriate height and complies with local regulations.
- **Action:** Trim overgrown vegetation that may obstruct the view of the fence.

9. Check for Leaning or Bowing:

- **Indicators:** Look for signs of leaning or bowing, especially after severe weather events.
- **Action:** Reinforce or replace any sections that are leaning or bowing.

10. Inspect the Bottom of the Fence:

- **Focus:** Check for gaps or spaces at the bottom of the fence.
- **Action:** Ensure that the fence is flush with the ground to prevent unauthorized access.

11. Evaluate Visibility:

- **Consideration:** Ensure that the fence allows visibility for security reasons.
- **Action:** Trim bushes or trees that may obstruct the view of the fence from the street or neighboring properties.

12. Address Discoloration or Stains:

- **Indicators:** Discoloration or stains may indicate mold or mildew growth.
- **Action:** Clean and treat the fence to prevent further growth and maintain its appearance.

13. Check the Fence Foundation:

- **Focus:** Ensure that the foundation of the fence is stable.
- **Action:** Repair any issues with the foundation to maintain the structural integrity of the fence.

14. Reinforce Security Features:

- **Check:** If the fence has security features, such as spikes or anti-climbing measures, ensure they are intact.
- **Action:** Repair or replace any security features that are damaged or missing.

15. Consider Future Upgrades:

- **Assessment:** Evaluate whether the current fencing meets your security and aesthetic needs.
- **Action:** Plan for upgrades if necessary, considering materials, height, and additional security features.

Regular and proactive inspection and maintenance of your property's fencing are essential to ensure its effectiveness in providing security, maintaining aesthetics, and contributing to the overall safety of your home. Addressing issues promptly can prevent more extensive and costly repairs in the future.

Checking for debris or obstructions behind your fence is a crucial step in maintaining a safe and secure outdoor environment. Accumulated debris can lead to various issues, including structural damage, pest infestations, and potential fire hazards. Here's a guide on how to ensure your neighbors haven't piled up debris behind your fence:

**1. Visual Inspection:

- **Frequency:** Conduct regular visual inspections of the area behind your fence.
- **Purpose:** Identify any signs of debris or objects that might have been piled up by neighbors.

**2. Open Communication:

- **Approach:** Politely communicate with your neighbors.
- **Discussion:** Inquire if they have any plans for the area behind your fence and express your concerns about debris accumulation.

**3. Maintain Neighboring Relationships:

- **Building Rapport:** Establish and maintain positive relationships with your neighbors.
- **Benefits:** A good relationship encourages open communication and mutual respect, making it easier to address concerns.

**4. Legal Boundaries:

- **Know Your Property Lines:** Be aware of your property lines and the legal boundaries between your property and your neighbors'.
- **Documentation:** Consult property surveys or legal documents to clarify boundaries.

**5. Provide Clear Information:

- **Share Concerns:** If you notice debris, inform your neighbors of the potential issues it may cause.
- **Collaboration:** Work together to find a solution that benefits both parties.

**6. Offer Assistance:

- **Help with Cleanup:** If your neighbors are willing, offer assistance with cleaning up the debris.
- **Collaboration:** Collaborative efforts can strengthen neighborly relations and maintain a clean shared space.

**7. Fencing Maintenance:

- **Regular Checks:** Include the area behind your fence in your regular fencing maintenance routine.
- **Prompt Action:** Address any debris promptly to prevent potential issues.

**8. Consider Landscaping Solutions:

- **Landscaping Barrier:** Propose the installation of a low-maintenance landscaping barrier between properties.
- **Benefits:** This can prevent debris accumulation and enhance the aesthetic appeal of the shared space.

**9. Documentation and Records:

- **Keep Records:** Document instances of debris accumulation with photographs.
- **Records for Reference:** Keep these records for reference in case legal assistance is needed.

**10. Local Regulations:

- **Research Local Laws:** Be aware of local ordinances and regulations regarding property maintenance.
- **Compliance:** Ensure that your neighbors comply with these regulations.

**11. Mediation Services:

- **Third-Party Mediation:** If communication breaks down, consider involving a neutral third party.
- **Resolution:** Mediation services can help find amicable solutions to property-related disputes.

**12. Legal Recourse:

- **Legal Consultation:** In extreme cases, seek legal advice if communication and mediation fail.
- **Understanding Rights:** Understand your rights and options for addressing property-related issues.

Conclusion:

Maintaining open communication with neighbors, conducting regular inspections, and addressing concerns promptly are key steps in ensuring that debris accumulation behind your fence does not compromise the safety and integrity of your property. Collaborative efforts and a proactive approach can lead to effective solutions that benefit both parties.